PASTA!

ACADEMIA
BARILLA

WHITE STAR PUBLISHERS

TEXT
ACADEMIA BARILLA

PHOTOGRAPHS
CHATO MORANDI

GENERAL COORDINATION
ILARIA ROSSI

INTRODUCTIONS
GUIDO, LUCA AND PAOLO BARILLA
GIANLUIGI ZENTI
MASSIMO BOTTURA
SCOTT CONANT

GRAPHIC DESIGN
MARINELLA DEBERNARDI

EDITORIAL STAFF
LAURA ACCOMAZZO

CONTENTS

EGG PASTA — 188

THE FASCINATING, MILLENARIAN HISTORY OF PASTA RUNS THROUGH THE WHOLE OF ITALY FROM NORTH TO SOUTH AND FROM COAST TO COAST. FROM THE FIRST REFERENCES IN ETRUSCAN AND ROMAN TIMES, TO FRESH PASTA, TO MEDIEVAL TESTIMONIES OF DRIED PASTA LINKED TO SICILY WHICH, AT THE TIME, WAS HEAVILY INFLUENCED BY ARAB CULTURE, TO RENAISSANCE DOCUMENTS, TO THE FIRST LITERARY QUOTATIONS AND THE FOUNDATION OF THE PASTA MANUFACTURERS IN LIGURIA AND NAPLES, ITALY HAS BEEN INEXTRICABLY LINKED WITH PASTA AND CONTINUES TO LIVE THROUGH PROGRESSIVE TRANSFORMATIONS AS A RESULT OF THE RECIPROCAL INFLUENCE OF TASTES AND PRODUCTIVE TECHNOLOGY.

BECAUSE ITALIAN PASTA IS THE PRODUCT OF TECHNOLOGY – THE DIE EXTRUSION TECHNOLOGY – IT IS THE RESULT OF THE INVENTIVENESS AND THE CREATIVITY OF MANY PLAYERS: PASTA MAKERS, INVENTORS AND COOKS HAVE ALL TOGETHER WRITTEN SIGNIFICANT PAGES IN ITS HISTORY.

THE HISTORY OF OUR FAMILY'S ASSOCIATION WITH PASTA GOES BACK A LONG WAY. THERE ARE RECORDS IN PARMA OF A CERTAIN OVIDIUS BARILLA, A MASTER BAKER OF THE CITY, DATING BACK TO 1553. HIS EXPERIENCE AND SKILLS WERE HANDED DOWN FROM GENERATION TO GENERATION, UNTIL 1877, WHEN, ALONG THE MAIN ROAD OF SAN MICHELE, PIETRO BARILLA SENIOR OPENED HIS BREAD AND PASTA STORE, THE FIRST NUCLEUS OF WHAT WOULD BECOME THE BARILLA ENTERPRISE, WHICH IS TODAY A WORLD LEADER IN ITALIAN PASTA AND AMBASSADOR OF ITALIAN CUISINE IN MORE THAN ONE HUNDRED COUNTRIES. WE HAVE BEEN MAKING PASTA FOR MORE THAN ONE HUNDRED AND THIRTY YEARS: IN ORDER TO WITHSTAND THE PASSING OF TIME IT IS NECESSARY TO HAVE FIRM ROOTS AND A STRONG PRODUCT CULTURE. A CULTURE WHICH WE ENJOY SHARING WITH OTHERS. THEREFORE, FOR US, TALKING ABOUT PASTA IS LIKING TALKING ABOUT OUR LIVES. THIS EXTRAORDINARY PRODUCT, CAPABLE OF BRINGING HEALTH AND WELL-BEING AND ADAPTING TO THE CUISINES OF ALL COUNTRIES, IS A VITAL PART OF OUR HISTORY AND OF OUR PRESENT.

THE PASTA THAT WE PRODUCE IS AT OUR TABLE. BUT TOGETHER WITH IT, THERE IS EVEN THE HISTORY OF OUR FAMILY AND THAT OF ALL THE OTHER CRAFTSMEN WHO, OVER THE CENTURIES, HAVE LOVED IT AND HELPED IT TO GROW WITH OUR COUNTRY. A COUNTRY THAT FOR CENTURIES WAS FRAGMENTED INTO DOZENS OF SMALL STATES (AND CUISINES), THAT HAS BECOME A NATION, AND THAT TODAY RECOGNIZES PASTA AS ITS NATIONAL DISH. BUT PASTA IS THE "QUEEN" OF MEDITERRANEAN EATING HABITS. AND MEDITERRANEAN DOES NOT ONLY MEAN ITALIAN; IT REPRESENTS THE USES AND CUSTOMS

OF AN ANCIENT CIVILIZATION, WHICH HAS ROOTS IN A MILD AND SUNNY LAND, RICH IN CEREALS, WHERE CULINARY HABITS ARE HANDED DOWN UNTIL THEY BECOME TRADITION. TODAY THERE IS NO NEED TO EXPLAIN THE NUTRITIONAL QUALITIES OF PASTA. ON THE CONTRARY, ONE WONDERS HOW IT COMES ABOUT, IN AN ERA OF "WORLDWIDE MARKETING," THAT A TYPICALLY ITALIAN FOOD HAS BECOME SO "UNIVERSAL" AND FAMOUS. THIS IS WHERE THE "PARADOX" OF PASTA LIES: THE FACT THAT IN IT, MODERNITY AND INNOVATION COINCIDE WITH TRADITION AND HEALTHY LIVING.

LEAFING THROUGH THE PAGES OF THIS BOOK THEREFORE IS NOT JUST AN EXERCISE IN BECOMING ACQUAINTED WITH RECIPES, PREPARATIONS, SAUCES OR LEARNING ABOUT CURIOSITIES ASSOCIATED WITH THE HISTORY AND THE PRODUCTION TECHNIQUES OR THE PRESENCE OF PASTA IN ITALIAN CULTURE: IT IS, INDEED A JOURNEY MADE UP OF MEN, FLAVORS, RESPECT FOR TRADITION BUT ALSO OF CONTINUOUS INNOVATION, OF SHARING AND FAMILY LOVE, OF THE PAST AND THE FUTURE.

GUIDO, LUCA AND PAOLO BARILLA

ACADEMIA BARILLA

THE WORLD'S AMBASSADOR FOR ITALIAN GASTRONOMY

PARMA, ONE OF THE CAPITALS OF ITALIAN CUISINE, IS NOTED THROUGHOUT THE WORLD FOR ITS LONG TRADITION OF HIGH-QUALITY FOOD AND AGRICULTURAL PRODUCTION. TYPICAL PRODUCTS FROM THE AREA, SUCH AS ITS PARMIGIANO-REGGIANO CHEESE AND THE COLD CUTS PROSCIUTTO DI PARMA AND CULATELLO, ALONG WITH CERTAIN TYPES OF PASTAS, ARE APPRECIATED INTERNATIONALLY. TODAY THE BARILLA CENTER CAN BE FOUND RIGHT IN THE CENTER OF THE CITY, A MULTIFUNCTION COMPLEX DESIGNED BY ARCHITECT RENZO PIANO, WHO RESTORED THE INDUSTRIAL AREA THAT ONCE WAS OCCUPIED BY BARILLA'S HISTORICAL PASTA-MAKING PLANT.

SINCE 2004, THE BARILLA CENTER HAS ALSO BEEN HOST TO THE ULTRAMODERN STRUCTURE OF ACADEMIA BARILLA, AN INTERNATIONAL CENTER DEDICATED TO SAFEGUARDING AND DEFENSE OF THE ITALIAN GASTRONOMICAL PATRIMONY FROM IMITATIONS AND COUNTERFEITING, TO THE PROMOTION AND DISTRIBUTION OF EXCELLENT QUALITY PRODUCTS, AND TO THE ENHANCEMENT OF THE ROLE OF ITALIAN FOOD SERVICES IN THE WORLD.

ACADEMIA BARILLA IS A MEETING PLACE FOR GREAT PROFESSIONALS OF THE KITCHEN AND FOR ENTHUSIASTS OF ITALIAN GASTRONOMY, WHERE UNIQUE CAPABILITIES AND OUTSTANDING PRODUCTS COME TOGETHER TO OFFER SERVICES RANGING FROM TRAINING COURSES TO GASTRONOMICAL TOURS.

EQUIPPED WITH A SPECTACULAR AUDITORIUM, A POLYSENSORIAL LABORATORY, VARIOUS TEACHING CLASSROOMS, AND AN INSIDE RESTAURANT, ACADEMIA BARILLA ALSO BOASTS A RICH GASTRONOMICAL LIBRARY, COMPRISING OVER 9000 VOLUMES AND A PRECIOUS COLLECTION OF HISTORICAL MENUS AND PRINTS, WHICH CAN EASILY BE CONSULTED ON THEIR INTERNET SITE.

ACADEMIA BARILLA ALSO OFFERS A VAST RANGE OF COURSES, MODULATED BASED ON THEME AND LEVEL OF COMPETENCY: CHEFS OF INTERNATIONAL RENOWN MAKE UP THE PRESTIGIOUS TEAM OF DOCENTS THROUGH WHOM THE HIGH-LEVEL EDUCATIONAL OFFERING IS PROPOSED. PERSONALITIES SUCH AS ETTORE BOCCHIA, MORENO CEDRONI, SCOTT CONANT, CARLO CRACCO, ALFONSO IACCARINO, GIADA DE LAURENTIIS, VALENTINO MARCATTILII, IGINIO MASSARI, GIANCARLO PERBELLINI, ANDREA ZANINI ENHANCE EACH MEETING WITH THEIR OWN RICH EXPERIENCE.

AWARDED THE PREMIO IMPRESA-CULTURA ("ENTERPRISE-CULTURE AWARD") IN 2007 FOR ITS ACTIVITY IN PROMOTING GASTRONOMIC CULTURE AND ITALIAN CREATIVITY THROUGHOUT THE WORLD, ACADEMIA BARILLA HAS FURTHERMORE ESTABLISHED THE PREMIO CINEMA ("AWARD CINEMA"), WITH THE PURPOSE OF DIFFUSING AWARENESS OF ITALIAN GASTRONOMIC CULTURE THROUGH THE MEANS OF SHORT FILMS.

GIANLUIGI ZENTI

MORE PASTA, PLEASE

Everyday at noon I'd call out to the guys on the beach with a megaphone from the campground: "Sello! Pasta anyone? Amatriciana or carbonara?" Palinuro, August 1980.

I've always been the cook of the group. With a few coins in my pocket and a pot of boiling water I was convinced that I had reached the height of my culinary expression that summer. I never dreamed of being a chef until I actually became one. Be careful what you wish for. It might come true.

My passion for the kitchen began with pasta. It began with Nonna Ancella's handmade egg pasta. She was a maverick rolling out pasta dough two times a day to please us with a plate of fresh tagliatelle, maltagliati or tortellini for lunch and dinner. My brothers and I were always hungry, eager and determined. I vividly remember my grandmother rolling out the dough with an expression on her face akin to joy. In her hands, the dough took on a life of its own flying like a translucent yellow sheet and illuminating those dark rooms closed off from the summer's heat. You need small fingers to fold tortellini and cut pasta dough properly; childrens' and grandmother's they say are the best. The former for their agility, the latter for their maturity. Under certain porticos just outside the city walls, women continue to fold tortellini surrounded by chatter, dogs, chickens and grandchildren running wild and free. These moments around the table served to reinforce my character, I was told. Look where I am now, still around that table.

How humble pasta can be. Served in abundance it is a meal. Quick, pleasing, friendly and comforting never gets old. How varied pasta can be from north to south, east to west. Discovering a new recipe, a filling, a ragù variation and the infinite combinations of ingredients in any given pasta dish is always a treasure. How generous pasta can be. At times it almost seems like it is evolving with us, changing based on our needs, habits, and tastes. It is flexible, it bends, it transforms, and goes to all ends to keep us in its company.

Pasta knows no confines. It flourishes in the most inhospitable places. The desire to make a "good plate" of pasta for a group of friends never wanes no matter how well you cook or where you call home. Besides, it is almost guaranteed that no one will ever say, "No" and the plates will come back clean.

"Charlie! Are you ready for pasta? All'amatriciana or carbonara?" Modena, June 2010

Massimo Bottura

AHH, PASTA!!!

Ahh, Pasta!!! Where does one start when discussing this simple, comforting, famous child of Italy? Well, I think it starts with passion. Italians are wildly passionate about their pasta. Every Italian has grown up eating what they believe is the best. Pasta is one of the most popular foods in the world and Italians are fully aware of that fact. Personally, the effects that pasta has had in my life are as broad as the spectrum of Italian cuisine itself. The warm memories of my grand-mother making cavatelli on her huge wooden pasta board are the foundation that I have set my career goals on. The taste memory of eating the first Tortelli in Brodo as a teenager outside of Bologna has stuck with me until this very moment. Seeing the light in a young cooks eyes, as he or she contemplates the textures and flavors of a beautiful bowl of pasta is something that I love to witness, knowing that their experience has raised the bar for them as they move forward in their careers. The list and experiences are countless. But the result of each story is the same; the depth of the experience matched the intensity of the passion put forth in the food.

Make no mistake; pasta is the most humble of products. But from its very meek starting point, it can be held in the highest regard. Pasta's simplicity is where its inherent beauty lies. One of the first things I teach someone to make is also the most difficult — spaghetti with garlic and oil. The balance of flavor, the proper cooking time of the pasta, the right amount of olive oil, the cooking of the garlic, why its imperative that no cheese is added... I can go on and on. What makes it special is the restraint, the love and the deep understanding of the products themselves.

As I think of the dialogue and various exchange of ideas I have shared with customers, clients and friends over the years, pasta has always been the subject first breached by them. Italy's love affair with pasta has truly arrived stateside. There are literally dozens of recipes all over Italy used for cooking the same dishes. The common thread for all of them is a very soulful and loving approach to each plate. The honesty of the product, the integrity and the technique all have to be flawless in order to achieve a superior final result. This book speaks directly to Italy's deep culinary history. It includes the best chefs from all over the country and their exploration of Italy's preferred dish which holds the space for setting a new standard, a new level of expectation from the most modest of ingredients.

Scott Conant

16

PASTA'S TIMELINE

THE ORIGINS OF PASTA

The history of pasta is lost in the mists of time: Its origins date back to when man began to abandon his nomadic hunter-gatherer lifestyle, characterized by frequent jaunts in search of wild seeds and fruits.

It was a time when he learned how to sow seeds and to wait for his labors to yield fruit, and when he learned the crude techniques required to change the look and taste of his food through the processing of these raw materials. The encounter with cereals and more specifically with their flours (and with the varying ways in which they can be used) created profound changes in the food culture of many peoples.

Almost all food historians of note agree that one of the earliest forms of refined foods for human consumption was a mixture of raw cereal grains crushed and mixed with water and then cooked.

This mixture was the ancestor of dough, which we can reasonably define as a food of mankind, rather than an invention of this or that nation.

Documented traces of this "primitive pasta" have evolved in parallel form, both from the Mediterranean basin and from continental Asia. But it was in the Mediterranean that pasta developed into the form that we know today.

From this primordial mixture, three basic categories of foods resulted: baked breads; gruels obtained by cooking the whole grains in water and then crushing them; and the pastas of different production techniques and origins, cooked either fresh or dried.

By the first millennium BC, the Greeks had already defined the wide, thin strips of pasta obtained from dough by the term *laganon*, before then passing the word on to Latin, where *laganum* stood for something much closer to our modern lasagna.

Wheat dough was made with ground wheat mixed with water or oil and spread into thin cakes, then cooked over burning stones to represent perhaps the first elementary processing of this food. The "galleys" of the Greek sailors, sung about by Homer in the Odyssey, had to be equipped for this type of cooking.

This method of working the dough, even with the various adjustments according to individual geographical areas, is still what today's household would consider "rolling dough," obtained from wheat flour mixed with eggs. This is the source of all the tapered pasta shapes: *lasagne, tagliatelle, tagliolini, maltagliati*, in addition to the pasta used to "package" stuffed pastas.

The North African descendants of the ancient Egyptians, who grew wheat along the banks of the Nile, still use wheat flour or semolina in many of their dishes. Originally, it was a way to store and transport their food, to protect it from pests and environmental changes as their caravans moved from place to place. It was here, in all probability, that pasta was dried for the first time under the desert sun. They created a food that would remain edible for a long time and despite difficult weather conditions; and it was a food that was easy to prepare once you reached one of the oases that dotted the caravan trails.

In the first known book about Arab cuisine, written by Ibran'al Mibrad and dating from the ninth century, various types of dried pasta were described and a preparation was suggested that is still found in some regions of the Middle East, for example in the Lebanon and Syria. Known as "Risto," it combines pasta, beans, and lentils and was widespread among the Bedouin and Berber populations.

19 • STAGES IN THE HARVESTING OF WHEAT IN ANCIENT EGYPT. TOMB OF MENNA, LUXOR.

It appears that it was under the influence of the Arabs, between the 11th and the 13th centuries, that pasta in its dried form came to be produced and consumed in Sicily. However, very recent studies undertaken by Emilio Milano suggest that the Jews also played an important part in the bringing of pasta-making techniques to the island. By the 1st century AD, they had established significant communities on the coast and inland, having been attracted by the commercial possibilities offered by this strategically placed island. According to the historian Maurice Aymard it was really the Jews who encouraged and organized the production of pasta on the island, helping to perpetuate the Arab-Norman culinary tradition in Sicily.

In any case, pasta's first capital, thanks to the knowledge of production methods, was Palermo in Italy (or more precisely Sicily).

By the twelfth century under the Normans, Sicilian pastas had begun to spread to the nearby southern regions. Around 1150 the Arab geographer Al-Idrisi (c. 1100–1165) documented the production of dry pasta in Trabia, not far from Palermo: 'tria' (a word derived from the Greek, from 'thrya' – thread-like rushes) was the name given to its pasta and the chronicler noted it was exported not only to nearby Calabria, but also to Christian and Muslim countries across the Mediterranean. Even today, the linguistic root of this term can still be recognized in some recipes in the local dialect where it indicates pasta. 'Tria' appears not only in Sicily but also in Salento, Barese and Ancona, all regions that have sizeable Jewish communities.

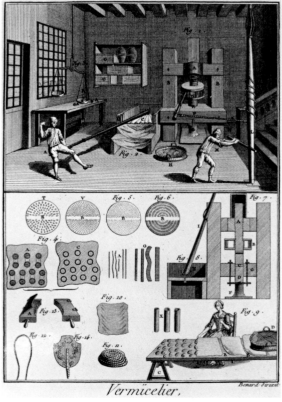

20 • TWO PLATES FROM THE ENCYCLOPEDIA OF DIDEROT AND D'ALEMBERT SHOWING THE PRODUCTION OF PASTA (17TH CENTURY).

In fifteenth-century Sicily, the distribution of pasta had reached such a point that the price became controlled and in the first half of that century a distinction was made between *vermicelli*, that is to say, the pasta from durum wheat, and the less valuable *macaroni*, pasta made from wheat flour.

At the beginning of the thirteenth century, the production and marketing of pasta spread to the region of Liguria; the Genoese merchants had got to know and appreciate the *tria* of Palermo, traveling to Sicily to import the original.

There are some unique documents in archives which record the production of pasta in Liguria as far back as the twelfth century; specifically, the existence of certain sizes and types of pasta are noted: *smooth pastas*, *macaronis*, and *lasagnas*.

In Liguria, a local dialect word 'fidei', probably of Spanish derivation, is often used to mean pasta. The producers of Ligurian pasta officially become a corporation, with their own statutes, in 1574. Following incorporation the constitution of the corporation was established: "the Rules of the Art of the Fidelari Masters." This was some years before the Neapolitan Corporation (1579) and, indeed, almost thirty years before the original capital of pasta, Palermo, saw its own producers incorporated (1605).

Neapolitans did not inherit the title of *macaroni eaters* from Palermo until the eighteenth century. Despite pasta arriving in Naples from Sicily in the fifteenth century, it was considered a luxury food, and the use of wheat and flour was also banned in times of crisis (... "war, famine or seasonal illness") during which the price of raw materials increased.

It is only from the sixteenth century onwards that we can begin to identify a number of locations in Campania, predominantly located on the Amalfi Coast, where the mills were situated thanks to the availability of water courses. Here the production of pasta flourished, so that optimal conditions for the production of a perfect product could be found. In addition to Naples, the names of some of these places – Gragnano and Torre Annunziata – (which became important in the mid-nineteenth century with the development of its craft factories) – still remain in the collective memories of pasta *aficionados*, especially foreign ones, as being synonymous with Italian pasta.

Pasta may have reached Italy via contact between the Northern Africans and the Sicilian people, but the way it spread into popular awareness was prompted by Naples and its culture. As is frequently shown in the iconography of the era, macaroni became (at least from the turn of the eighteenth century), "street food," cooked and sold in kiosks on street corners with no garnish or seasoned with pepper and grated cheese. It was also in Naples, several centuries after its first arrival in Italy, that its most memorable union occurred, the one with the tomato *l'americano* that would occur only during the late nineteenth century.

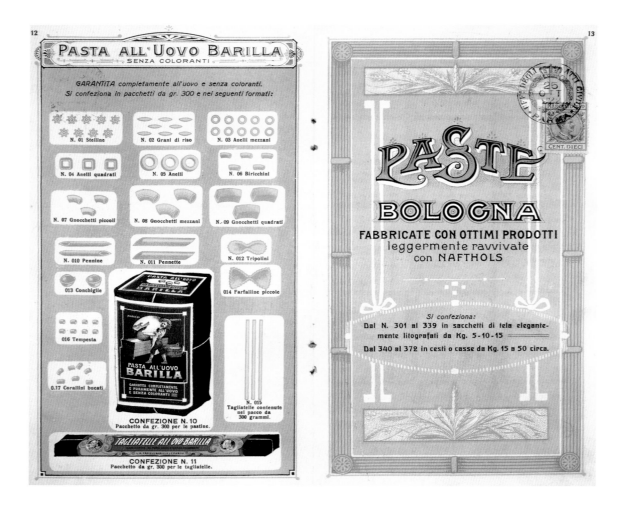

Even the appearance of pasta, from its beginnings until the present day, has evolved, although the progression has been rather a gradual one. In modern homes and artisanal production, you will still find the products of those formats first made exclusively by hand or with the first simple tools, such as the rolling pin. Therefore, we enjoy *gnocchi* and *gnocchetti*, *orecchiette*, *cavatieddi*, *troffie*, whose shapes are formed with the fingers or rolling pins used to roll the dough. Which were the first pastas obtained with these simple tools? The family of lasagnas, descendants of the ancient Roman *lagane* products: *tagliatelle, tagliolini, taglierini, fettucce, fettuccine...* that in some regions, in recognition of their delicious flavor, became known as *pappardelle* or *paparelle* (from the popular verb *pappare* – to scoff)!

Even small types of pasta, which are obtained by cutting shapes, underwent subsequent manual handling: butterflies or *stricchetti* (by the fingers that hold the center of the piece of dough; *garganelli*, squares rolled over themselves into a quill shape; and *corzetti*, pasta rounds decorated with a stencil.

From decorative prints came the notion not only of producing shapes manually, but of producing a consistent shape with a mould. With this logical step, pasta production migrated from the common kitchen to artisanal production with the help of specially designed machines. Presses began to

PASTE NAPOLI
della lunghezza di centimetri 60 circa.

501 Vermicelli *35 45*

502 Spaghettini *36 44*

503 Spaghetti *37 44*

504 Bucatini *38 44*

505 Maccaroncelli *39 46*

506 Mezzanelli *40 44*

507 Mezzani *41 48*

508 Zite *42 44*

509 Zitoni *43 44*

510 Linguine

511 Fetuccine *44 44*

512 Fetucce

PASTE NAPOLI
della lunghezza di centimetri 60 circa.

513 Reginette a doppio riccio

514 Reginette

515 Lasagne

516 Lasagnoni

PASTE GENOVA
I numeri 445 - 446 - 447 si fabbricano nella lunghezza di 8 cm. circa.

445 Parigini bucati

446 Sprochetti

447 Maccheroni

448 Maniche elettriche

449 Mezze maniche liscie piccole *13*

450 Maniche liscie *19*

451 Mezze maniche liscie grosse *14*

452 Maniche liscie grosse *20*

453 Mezze maniche rigate *25*

454 Maniche rigate *28*

PASTE GENOVA

455 Minutini fini

456 Minutini Mezzani

457 Spaghetti

548 Bucatini a matassa

459 Bavettine

22 AND 23 • SOME PAGES FROM THE 1916 BARILLA CATALOG SHOWING TYPES OF PASTA STILL BEING CHARACTERIZED IN ACCORDANCE WITH PLACE OF ORIGIN: LONG FROM NAPLES; SHORT FROM GENOA; EGG-BASED FROM BOLOGNA.

produce pastas that were "drawn" through them (hence the name given to the perforated disc placed at the head of press: *trafila*). These moulds were the subject of passionate study and true artistry by *trafilai*, skilled craftsmen, who were able to create and refine through the use of different materials (first copper, then bronze and steel, with other materials present), a tool that, over the years, has allowed us to achieve an endless variety of superior quality pasta.

There are still many who think that pasta is of Chinese origin, as recounted by Marco Polo (1254–1324) in his travel memoirs "Milione" dictated at the end of the thirteenth century to Rustichello, who then transcribed them into French in "Le divisement du monde." Although, as we have seen, the discovery of pasta followed a parallel evolution, one which was also Eastern and Chinese, the concept that it came to Italy from China is a myth.

Marco Polo, in speaking of the kingdom of Fansur, a South-East Asian island, states: "They have no wheat... but to my great surprise, they have a 'flour tree' which is large and yields a soft husk. These trees are plentiful and all filled with meal which is good and eaten a lot. I often ate it." The original French text states that the inhabitants of that island "do not have wheat or other grains." The tree mentioned by Marco Polo is the sago tree, the popular name of palm trees of the Cycas and Caryota genus, which yields a starchy food. In the first Italian version publication of "Milione," Giovan Battista Ramusio (1485–1557) added the following note: "...the meal was cleaned and washed, adopted and made into lasagna, pasta and other dishes, which Marco Polo said he had eaten more than once. He also brought some dried meal with him back to Venice, and its taste is like that of barley bread..."

Giuseppe Prezzolini, writing in the 1930s, explains the misconception that noodles were imported from China: "in America, they have not hesitated to take the text of Ramusio to heart... and have concluded that this is the proof." It was from America that the legend of pasta's Chinese provenance would spread throughout the world. In fact, at the time of the voyage of Marco Polo, pasta had been known in Italy for centuries and it was unquestionably the Italians who invented the press and the die, essential tools in the production of pasta from durum wheat and semolina.

Thanks to the initiative of some individual entrepreneurs who came from these areas or who had traveled there specially to learn, pasta dough began to spread into the interior from the large centers of Italian pasta making. Historical evidence, dating back as early as the end of the thirteenth century, documents its appearance in Florence, Milan, Cremona, Lodi, and Venice. That is without forgetting the Sardinian *maccheroni* and Roman *vermicelli*. It was thanks to technology that the spread of pasta across the world really accelerated. Moving from artisanal production to proto-industrial and then to full industrial production, the product spread into the areas that did not originally show the natural climatic conditions for optimum drying. Thanks to technology, the most important elements of pasta production can be completely disengaged from the variables determined by climate and season, thus becoming a safer, more uniform industrial process as regards the final product.

Italian pasta began its "journey" into immortality with its export to other countries. Sicily and Genoa were famous for their exports and the product soon attracted the attention of other countries. Thomas Jefferson (1743–1826), who was destined, of course, to become the third president of the United States (1801 to 1809), sent an envoy to seek new approaches to agriculture and industry for his country while he was serving the young nation in Paris. In 1797, he sent William Short to Naples, where he succeeded in procuring a pasta press that was shipped to the United States. And it was Jefferson who collected and put into practice, for the first time in America, some recipes to cook macaroni. He even left a book of homemade recipes for cooking this Italian specialty that continued to be imported from its country of origin in large quantities until World War I.

A machine similar to that bought by Jefferson in Naples had already been imported from Italy into Switzerland. In 1731, the monks of the Benedictine monastery of Disentis installed a *torculum pro formandis macaronis*. This development allowed the pasta culture to spread slowly north of the Alps. It was not until the late eighteenth and early nineteenth centuries, however, when thousands of Swiss settled in Italy (especially in Naples), as soldiers, bankers, debt collectors, industrial textile magnates, and hoteliers, that pasta consumption really began to spread throughout the Confederation.

25 • ARTISANAL WORKING OF PASTA AT THE TORRE ANNUNZIATA (NAPLES) IN THE 1930S.

One of them, the engineer August von Wittel (early nineteenth century to 1857), a native of Thun in the canton of Berne, and his son Theodor, arrived in Campania as a technician for the Dubois Company working on the construction of the first Italian railway, the Naples–Portici line. August married Rosetta Inzerillo, the daughter of one of the most famous artisanal bakers of Torre Annunziata, and in turn, become a manufacturer of pasta. He transformed the little workshop into a veritable pasta powerhouse, which was further enlarged in 1879 by his son Giovanni, who had meanwhile "neapolitanized" his surname to Vojello. Today Vojello is a symbol of Neapolitan gastronomy, becoming part of the great Barilla family in 1973. Pietro Barilla Sr. (1845–1912) came from a family of bakers that had been in Parma, in the Po Valley, since 1553. In 1877, he opened his small shop specializing in bread and pasta, destined to become (after four generations and more than a century of business), the world leader in pasta, available in over 100 countries and four continents.

The Italian-style pasta dish is a homemade creation, the result of local products where available (wheat, eggs, vegetables, fish, meat, cheese) combined with a little knowledge and infinite variations. In different recipes, one can enjoy an array of supporting flavors. Popular wisdom has also produced combinations that are often nutritionally perfect. It is also no accident that pasta dishes have become acceptable as main dishes at a restaurant, and yet at the same time remain ideal for those occasions when you want to simplify the meal and save time.

But wherever you eat—at home, at a restaurant, at work or with friends—pasta is always a pleasure, seasoned with a thousand years of culinary experience and the imagination of many Italian chefs.

The production of dried pasta is made up of four stages: the mixing of ingredients; the kneading and refining of the dough; the formation of the different types of pasta; and the drying process. Over time, these phases have seen a progressive transformation in the way technology is used to complete them. In the coming pages, we shall follow the fascinating journey through history to the current ultra-modern facilities that produce our pasta.

The raw material, the semolina obtained from the milling of durum wheat, will undergo a preventative cleaning process to remove any residues or impurities by being sieved, a task that was originally handled manually, then mechanically.

After the preventative step, it is time to move on to the mixture. It is necessary to mix the right quantities of semolina and water; initially this was done manually with the use of the feet and later with special machines that allow greater processing hygiene. Secondly, one has to select the temperature of the water used for mixing the dough, which can vary from 59° to 77°F (from 15° to 25°C) and from 104° to 212°F (from 40° to 100°C), depending on whether "cold" or "hot" water is used. The choice is dictated by the quality of the semolina and by the likelihood that fermentation could develop during the drying process that would, ultimately, affect the final product.

For similar reasons, the mixing phase lasts no more than 5–20 minutes to prevent ruining the dough in the drying process.

At the beginning of the twentieth century, different types of mixers were built and used: small metal

D. BALLARI ROSSI O.
Parma - Italia

28 • COMPLETE INSTALLATION FOR A PASTA MAKING FACTORY, PRODUCED BY THE COMPANY BALLARI-ROSSI OF PARMA, WITH DOUGH MIXER IN THE FORE-GROUND, KNEADING MACHINE AND PRESS IN LINE, DATABLE TO THE 1890S.

mixers with a capacity of 10 to 60 lbs (4.5 to 27 kg) which required manual operation. These
were often equipped with a reversible tub into which one could empty the contents directly
ready to knead, performing the second stage of processing.

The mixers were adopted very quickly on an industrial scale. The production from the new
engines provided high machining accuracy and a better quality of the product: these machines could work two or three hundred pounds of dough.

Other technological improvements included the provision of mixers with a rotating stick-
shaft, which made it possible to keep the tub containing the mixture clean, thus preventing
the subsequent processes from being subjected to fermentation caused by residues that
were not removed.

The mixers in the old pasta factory were placed in an elevated position, upstream of the kneading machines, with which they had to work in sync. This allowed the time between the two jobs to
be optimized by preventing the dough from drying or allowing excessive fermentation to occur.

The next stage in the production of the dough is the mixing or kneading, which is undertaken to perfect the consistency of the dough, making it more compact and homogeneous, more elastic and durable and more uniform in color.

The first manual kneading was done with what is known as a "rolling pin": a long wooden baton worked using the arms to roll the dough. The dough is placed on a table or polished surface and rolled until it is soft enough. This method required a lot of muscle and effort to use.

At the same time, in Liguria especially, a technique similar to the technology used in mills was being utilized. The dough was in effect "milled" by a marble wheel or other stone in a circular motion to press it into a round basin, with continued pressure. This model of kneading presented a number of challenges due to the fact that the smooth wheel, without grooves, created a strong friction with the basin and tended to pummel the dough, making it whitish in appearance and fragile during cooking.

Rollers with grooves were perfected which allowed intermittent pressure to be exerted on the dough. Next to the "rolling pin" as the best innovation for kneading, was the introduction of "roller bearings" which has proved to be the best method for processing all types of dough. The kneading process with "roller bearings" consists of putting the dough in a circular tub that rotates on its axis while allowing two grooved, revolving rollers set in a rack to squeeze the dough through gradually. This in turn, can then be turned mechanically or by hand in the opposite direction.

The rolling concept also spawned another method for kneading, one using "blades." Formed of a wooden, circular table that slowly rotates on its axis, the dough is placed on top of the table and rhythmically worked over by wooden "blades" that are lowered onto the table.

Kneading has different processes according to location too: the Neapolitan method prefers the "blade," a close relative of the "pin," because it is at its best on hot dough. In Liguria and in some areas of the Veneto, the preferred means of kneading is "milling." The most common method remains, however, the "roller bearings."

30 • KNEADING MACHINE WITH CONICAL, CAST IRON ROLLERS, BY FRATELLI FRAVEGA OF MILAN, DATABLE TO AROUND THE TURN OF THE 20TH CENTURY.

31 • ILLUSTRATION DEPICTING A WOODEN KNEADING MACHINE IN A PASTA MAKING FACTORY, FROM *LA NUOVA ARCHITETTURA* BY ALESSANDRO CAPRA (BOLOGNA, 1678).

The next step in the process, which is not always followed if the pasta is a down-to-earth version, is the "forming" process that involves passing the dough through two smooth rollers to enhance the homogenous characteristics. This is done primarily to obtain thin sheets or specialty pastas, especially those containing eggs or those that need to be created manually from the dough.

Originally dough was formed exclusively via the "rolling" process, especially for the artisanal types, while the move to industrial production saw extrusion emerge as a method to form the pasta, forcibly passing it first through a copper stamp, then through a bronze one with holes cut to obtain the different forms and sizes of the finished product.

These metal stamps were mounted on the presses (horizontal or vertical) by a screw mechanism that enabled one to push the dough into a chamber and then through the press using arm

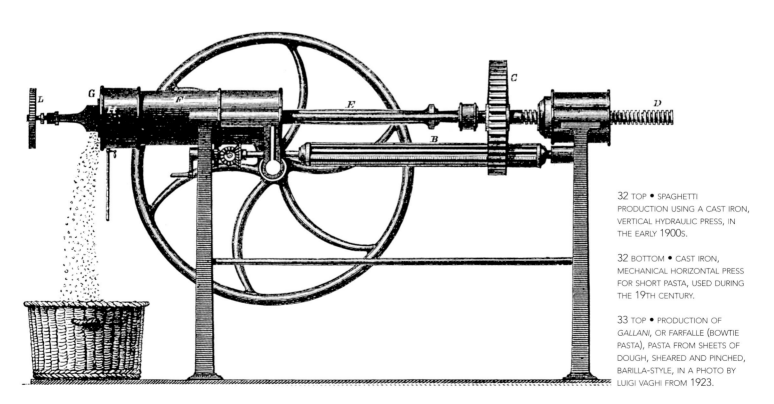

32 TOP • SPAGHETTI PRODUCTION USING A CAST IRON, VERTICAL HYDRAULIC PRESS, IN THE EARLY 1900s.

32 BOTTOM • CAST IRON, MECHANICAL HORIZONTAL PRESS FOR SHORT PASTA, USED DURING THE 19TH CENTURY.

33 TOP • PRODUCTION OF GALLANI, OR FARFALLE (BOWTIE PASTA), PASTA FROM SHEETS OF DOUGH, SHEARED AND PINCHED, BARILLA-STYLE, IN A PHOTO BY LUIGI VAGHI FROM 1923.

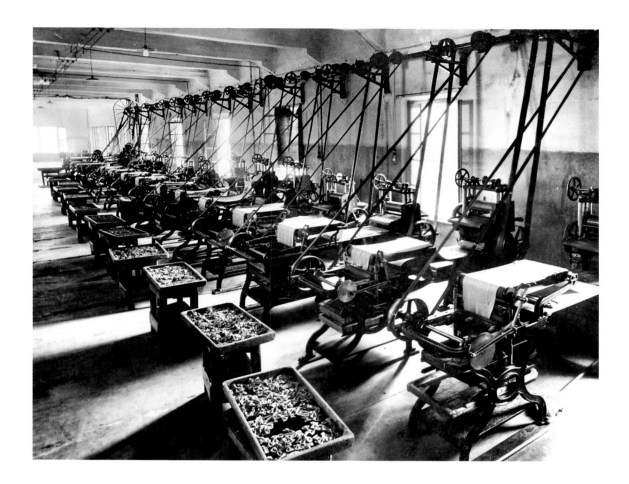

or engine power. Depending on the type of pasta, blades were placed at the exit of the press to cut the dough rhythmically as it exited. The holes of these dies also took into account the subsequent drying of pasta products, and thereby had a dimension that was 10 percent larger when compared to the desired shape.

In the long process of automating the pasta industry, the hydraulic press eventually replaced the manual "roller." The first models were built around 1870 by the Neapolitan firm Pattison. Although more expensive, they proved much more convenient in terms of production as with this kind of press one could work all sorts of dough, and even though the yield was better with the hot, soft dough, the mechanized efforts were often less complex and less subject to failure.

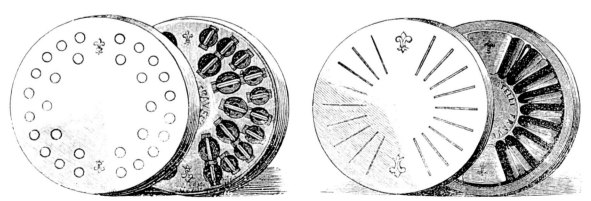

33 BOTTOM • SERIES OF FORMS OR DIES, IN A WOOD ENGRAVING FROM *CHIMICA DELLA VITA QUOTIDIANA* BY FRANCESCO REULEAUX (TURIN, 1899).

The pasta that comes from the press is spread manually on long form rods, though first it falls on a more rudimentary device, the *trabatto*, which shakes the pasta to air it in order to avoid clumping due to moisture and warping.

The pasta, spread out on these long rods or on "fat trays," then passes to the drying process, which is essential for the preservation and marketing of the product.

This, more than any other part of the process, took more application of knowledge and human observation. In the past, drying could only be done in the most favorable natural conditions. Hence the geographical location of the main production sites, mostly in coastal and marine areas, favored by the presence of intermittent breezes.

This phase, which became almost a "ritual," gave rise to professional roles that resembled witchcraft: the "Chief Pasta Maker" knew the seasons, the winds and knew that their changes would prevent the pasta from completing its magical alchemy. Knowledge like this (even from empirical evidence of this kind) was complex and plentiful, and made a real art of the role. The operation happened in stages.

A first drying took place in the sun in the courtyards or on terraces, hardening the surface of the pasta and giving it the texture of paper. A tempering stage followed, and took place instead in a cool cellar, where the remaining moisture in the pasta was permitted to redistribute evenly throughout the product. Final drying was done in well-oriented, large rooms with openings exposed to constant winds.

34 AND 35 • TWO LARGE, STATIC DRYING MACHINES FOR HANKS OF EGG PASTA AND FOR SPAGHETTI, IN OPERATION AT THE BARILLA PASTA MAKING FACTORY AROUND 1914, IN TWO PHOTOGRAPHS BY LUIGI VAGHI.

As in all processes closely related to natural conditions, it soon became evident that it was as important to avoid variability as much as ensuring these conditions.

Soon, people began to design and build artificial systems that involved the use of closed rooms equipped with mechanical ventilators and radiators to generate heat and breezes as required. Dating back to 1875, there were apparatuses used for this purpose: a cage of wood and iron on a polygonal plan, called "the carousel," rotated on its axis to give the pasta (rested on frames or reeds) an opportunity to dry. The drying of pasta in this fashion, however, was done imperfectly and it would be necessary to wait until 1898 before an artificial system (known as the *Tommasini* method) was tested that could reproduce the natural method. The first phase of this method took place in caissons heated to a temperature of 86–95°F (30–35°C) for a variable length of time of between 30 to 60 minutes, depending on the shape of the pasta. Then the pasta was put in rooms to diffuse the remaining moisture before ultimately being taken to the final drying chambers. In the latter, the ventilation was controlled artificially by a mechanism that made it possible to alternate regularly the speed of the tempering stage. Drying of short pasta could be completed in 24 hours, while long pasta took 3–6 days. Although this method brought considerable savings in time and space, the *Tommasini* method still required a large labor force.

It was not until the early twentieth century that we start to see the emergence of certain patents from R. Rovetta and G. Falchi, which realized the drying phases in a closed and artificial environment. Other important technological innovations for this phase of production were also introduced with the *Marelli* automatic dryer and the *Ceschina* drying chamber.

Each of these machines, now capable of replicating the common proto-industrial and artisanal production, lacked a further and final step: that of creating a continuous and com-

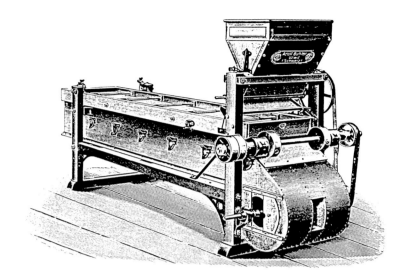

37 • THE FIRST "CONTINUOUS PRESS," CALLED THE MARSIGLIESE, REFINED BY IN FÉRÉOL SANDRAGNÉ 1917. IT SUBSTITUTED THE PISTON OF THE TRADITIONAL PRESS WITH AN ENDLESS SCREW, THUS BEGINNING THE PROCESS OF AUTOMATING PASTA PRODUCTION.

plete production cycle. Specifically, it lacked a cycle that would allow a factory to input the raw materials and churn out a safe, finished product with consistent quality.

To achieve this they would need new innovations that would help to automate some stages of production and bring them all together. The first continuous press was born of careful observation and the insight of Féréol Sandragné, a retired Mécanique Méridionale employee (a company that made machines for pasta factories, and had built the first mechanical coiler for "nest" pasta). Sandragné had found himself employed with a brick manufacturer, and being able to observe the machines with which they manufactured the raw bricks, built a prototype using the observed method: Two cogs, rotating continuously, pushed the clay through the shaped chain; the bricks that came out were then cut to size by a wire. This prototype was shown to his old employers who, after some refinements, released a Sandragné patent for his work (1917) and began producing the new continuous press after granting the inventor a percentage of each machine that was manufactured.

The innovation, which allowed a single machine to merge the various stages – dough-making, kneading and forming – was a great success and from 1929 to 1939 the French company produced almost one machine a day. The first continuous press of Italian production dates back to a project conceived by Parma engineers Giuseppe and Mario Braibanti in 1933.

Finally, it was necessary to provide for a successful drying process to achieve the goal of complete automation. For short pasta, frames were replaced with conveyors, which could move the product into different drying cells. The more complex problem of handling the long pasta was solved through rack or chain systems. The result of this long evolution is the modern pasta factory that, apart from production unimaginable to the craftsmen of old, has reached unsurpassed levels of hygiene and quality.

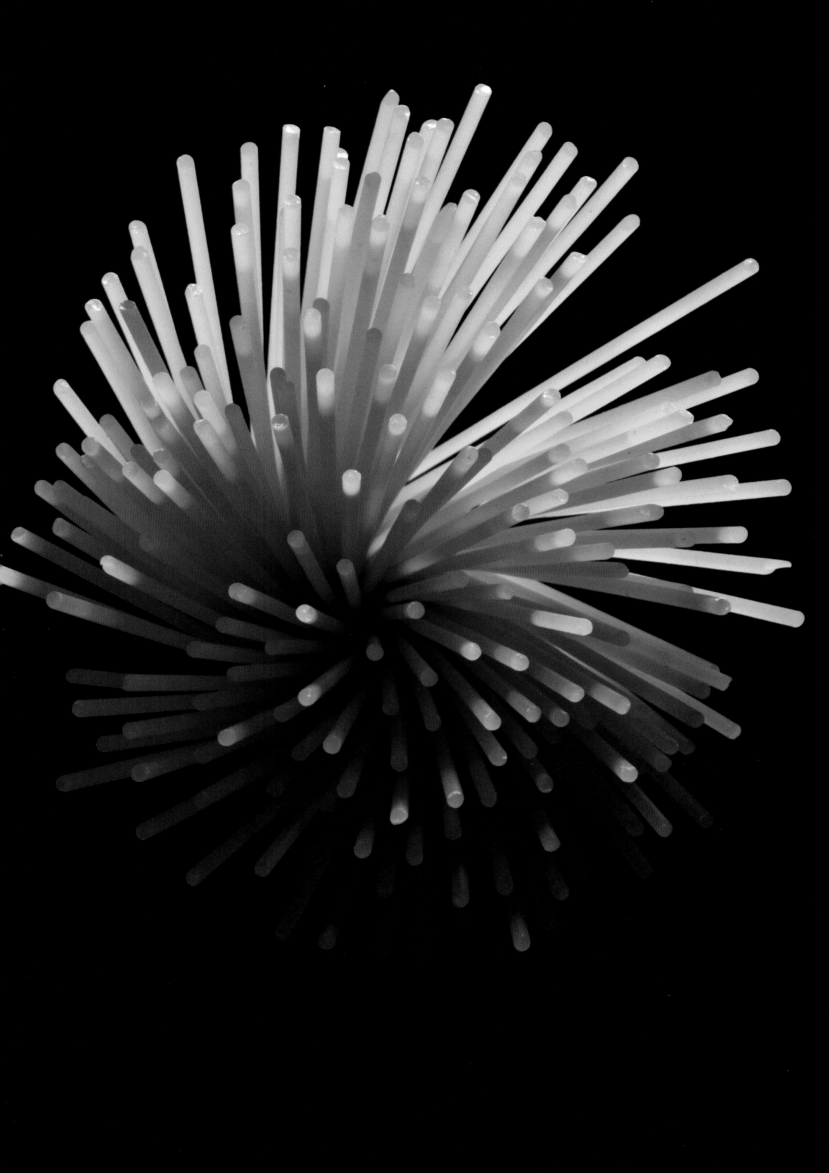

DURUM WHEAT
SEMOLINA PASTA

Pasta can be divided into two major types: dried pasta and fresh pasta. However, these definitions only refer to the drying process which makes the pasta keep better.

If we look at the ingredients of the dough, we should really divide pasta into the following types: durum wheat semolina pasta, egg pasta, filled pasta and specialty pasta.

Dried durum wheat semolina, as we know it today, was introduced into Sicily in the twelfth century during the Arab colonization, and then spread rapidly to Genoa and Naples between the thirteenth and sixteenth centuries. With the introduction of new drying technologies in the nineteenth century, it was then possible to extend pasta production across the entire country.

Pastas from durum wheat are now produced almost entirely on an industrial scale. The dough is made by mixing the semolina with water; the pasta shapes are produced by an extrusion mechanism, which forces the dough though shaping disks before it is cut to take on its virtually final form (it will be reduced in size further during the drying process, when its volume will become fixed as a long shelf-life, hard product).

The quality of this product is closely linked with the quality of the handful of essential raw materials. The most important of all are the durum wheat semolina, which is obtained by a meticulous grinding and sieving process, and water with optimal molecular characteristics. The manufacturing process is carefully controlled to give a product with a specific color and flavor which is then suitable for cooking.

Among the types of durum wheat pasta available, many can be traced back to the ancient cooking traditions of the various Italian regions. The easiest to distinguish are the "long pastas," although their sizes may vary: they may be rounded like spaghetti, vermicelli, capellini, or of different thickness; rounded with a hole in the center like bucatini, ziti, fusilli bucati; or oval or flat like bavette, linguine, tagliatelle and taglierini. The following examples of "short pastas" are among the most common; they may be smooth or ridged and include penne, rigatoni, maccheroni, mezze maniche, fusilli, eliche, and conchiglie. Many smaller sizes are found under the heading of "soup pasta"; these include anellini, ditalini, and stelline.

There are also formats that are defined by the extrusion process used in their manufacture: they include, for example, *farfalle*, also known as *stricchetti* for the characteristic way they are pinched in at the center. Finally, there are also some typically regional shapes produced by particular processes. One example is bigoli from Veneto, a sort of large-diameter forerunner of spaghetti that is extruded from a homemade tool; and then there are *trofie* from Liguria — gnocchi dough rolled and tempered at the ends that goes beautifully with pesto; and *corzetti*, Ligurian coin-shaped pasta that in former times used to carry the coat of arms for each family. Puglian *orecchiette* are small dumplings shaped like a squashed ear that are created using the blade of the knife as a spatula. *Malloreddus* from Sardinia are small dumplings across which a "comb" is dragged to form the shape; they are served with a rich tomato sauce and various meats. As for sauces, well that opens up a whole new world. As Giuseppe Prezzolini observed in his book on pasta; "there are more 'schools of thought' on sauces than there are on philosophy."

BAVETTE ALLA TRASTEVERINA
TRASTEVERE-STYLE BAVETTE

Difficulty 1

Ingredients for 4 people
Preparation time: 35' (preparation: 25' – cooking: 10')

14 oz (400 g) bavette
4 desalted anchovies
4 oz (100 g) drained tuna
4 oz (100 g) mushrooms
2 tbs (40 ml) extra virgin olive oil
2 cloves garlic
5 oz (150 g) tomatoes
1 tbs chopped parsley
½ oz (15 g) butter
Salt
Pepper

Method

Put half of the oil into a skillet with a clove of garlic. Remove the garlic as soon as the oil has heated up. Add 2 anchovies that have been rinsed and cut into small pieces and sauté lightly. Then add the tomatoes, previously blanched, skinned and seeded.

When the sauce starts to thicken, add the tuna which has been cut up into pieces on a chopping board; season with a little salt and plenty of pepper and leave to cook. Meanwhile, clean the mushrooms carefully and slice very thinly.

Heat a skillet with the rest of the oil and a clove of garlic, removing the clove just as it begins to color. Add the mushrooms, season with salt and pepper and cook over a high heat. When all the liquid has evaporated, place the butter in the skillet, blended with the remaining anchovies that have been well crushed with the blade of a knife.

Leave the pan on a moderate heat just as long as it takes for the butter to melt, and then add a heaped spoonful of chopped parsley. Cook the bavette in a large pan of lightly salted boiling water. Drain when *al dente* and dress with the prepared sauce and the mushrooms sprinkled over the top. Serve at once.

BAVETTE CON CATALOGNA E PATÉ DI OLIVE
BAVETTE WITH CHICORY AND OLIVE PATÉ

Difficulty 1

Ingredients for 4 people
Preparation time: 20' (preparation: 10' – cooking: 10')

14 oz (400 g) bavette
4 oz (100 g) endive
2 cloves chopped garlic
1½ oz (40 g) black olive paste
1½ oz (40 g) freshly grated Pecorino
2 tbs (30 ml) extra virgin olive oil
Salt
Pepper

Method

Wash and trim the endive. Boil in salted water for five minutes and drain. Cook the pasta in a large pot of salted boiling water. Meanwhile, heat the oil in a skillet over a medium heat and gently fry the garlic until just golden.

Add the endive and continue cooking for a few minutes. Stir in the olive paste. Cook the pasta in a large pan of lightly salted boiling water; drain when *al dente*. Combine with the prepared sauce and sprinkle with the grated Pecorino.

Olive paste is essentially the equivalent of tapenade, a Provençal spread made from black olives, oil, garlic, and aromatic herbs. It is easy to find commercially prepared varieties that can be used both as a pasta sauce and for canapés.

BUCATINI AL PECORINO E POMODORI

BUCATINI WITH PECORINO AND TOMATOES

Difficulty 1

Ingredients for 4 people
Preparation time: 40' (preparation: 15' – cooking: 25)

14 oz (400 g) bucatini
12 oz (350 g) tomatoes
1 tbs chopped parsley
1 onion
4 leaves basil
1 clove garlic
3 oz (80 g) shaved Pecorino
¼ cup (50 ml) extra virgin olive oil
Salt
Pepper

Method

Finely chop the basil, onion, and garlic. Heat the oil in a skillet over a moderate heat. Add the chopped ingredients and the parsley, and fry gently.

Cut the tomatoes into wedges, lengthwise, and break up with the prongs of a fork. Combine with the fried mixture. Season with salt and cook for 15 minutes.

Cook the pasta in a large pan of lightly salted boiling water. Drain when *al dente*. Dress with the prepared sauce and season with ground pepper. Place the pasta in an ovenproof dish, adding a little of the cooking water. Cover with the Pecorino and bake in the oven at 360°F (180°C) for 10 minutes. Turn out from the dish and divide into portions. Serve immediately.

BUCATINI ALL'AMATRICIANA
BUCATINI WITH AMATRICIANA SAUCE

Difficulty 1

Ingredients for 4 people
Preparation time: 27' (preparation: 15' – cooking: 12')

14 oz (400 g) bucatini
7 oz (200 g) pork cheek or smoked pancetta
4 ripe tomatoes
3 basil leaves
2 cloves garlic
1 (or 2 dried) fresh red chilli
2 tbs (40 ml) extra virgin olive oil
1½ oz (40 g) grated Pecorino
Salt
Pepper

Method

Cut the pork cheek into slices and then strips. Heat the oil in a skillet over a medium heat, add the pig's cheek or pancetta, and cook until the fat runs out.

In a pan of boiling water, blanch the tomatoes for 20 seconds, remove the skins and the seeds, and cut tomatoes into pieces. Chop the garlic and add to the skillet; cook for a few seconds. Tear the basil into pieces. Add the tomatoes, chilli, and basil, and season with salt and pepper. Cook for ten minutes.

Place the pasta in a large pan of lightly salted boiling water and drain when *al dente*. Dress with the prepared sauce and the Pecorino.

Italian Region: Lazio.

FOOD HISTORY

Amatriciana sauce takes its name from Amatrice, a small town in the Lazio region in the municipality of Rieti.
The use of tomato in the preparation distinguishes it from gricia, another sauce based on pork cheek (bacon) and pepper. The addition of tomato, linked to the use of long pasta such as "bucatini" (long, hollow tubular pasta) or spaghetti, is a traditional Italian custom: It was already attested in the early 1800s by the French gourmet Grimond de la Reynière in his "Almanach des Gourmands."
In Rome, Amatriciana sauce is normally served with "bucatini" and sprinkled with Pecorino Romano sheep's milk cheese, whereas in Amatrice it traditionally accompanies spaghetti.
Source: Academia Barilla Gastronomic Library.

BUCATINI ALLA CARUSO
BUCATINI CARUSO-STYLE

Difficulty 1

Ingredients for 4 people
Preparation time: 37' (preparation: 25' – cooking: 12')

14 oz (400 g) bucatini
10 oz (300 g) fresh or canned tomatoes
1 red or yellow bell pepper
2 cloves garlic
1 chilli
2 tbs (40 ml) extra virgin olive oil
1 pinch oregano
4 leaves basil
1 tbs chopped parsley
1 zucchino (courgette)
1 tbs flour
6½ cups (1.5 l) sunflower oil
Salt

Method

Heat the oil in a skillet over a medium heat. Quarter the garlic cloves, then fry them gently. Remove them when they begin to color. Chop the tomatoes and cut the peppers into chunks, place in the skillet. Turn up the heat and add the oregano, crushed chilli, and the basil to the sauce.

Slice the zucchino (courgette) into rounds, coat with flour, and deep-fry in hot oil. Cook the pasta in salted boiling water and drain when *al dente*. Dress with the prepared sauce, adding the fried zucchino slices and sprinkle with the chopped parsley.

Italian Region: Campania.

FOOD HISTORY

The recipe was created by the great tenor, who loved more than everything else the pasta typical of his native Naples. The story has it that, when he was once given a cool reception by his fellow-citizens, Caruso swore he would never sing in Naples again but he would return there only to enjoy his favorite pasta dish.

BUCATINI ALLA DOMENICANA
BUCATINI WITH MUSHROOMS

Difficulty 1

Ingredients for 4 people
Preparation time: 30' (preparation: 15' – cooking: 15')

14 oz (400 g) bucatini
4 salted anchovies
¼ cup (60 ml) extra virgin olive oil
2 oz (50 g) dried porcini mushrooms
2 cloves garlic
1 tbs parsley
2 oz (50 g) breadcrumbs
Salt
Pepper

Method

Soak the dried mushrooms in water, then chop them. Heat half the oil in a skillet over a medium heat, add the mushrooms and a little water, salt, and pepper. When the mushrooms are cooked, press them through a sieve, adding some of the liquid from the pan; put to one side.

Place the remainder of the oil in a skillet and cook the garlic until it begins to color, then remove it. Add the mushroom paste with the reserved liquid. Stir together for a minute, then remove from the heat. Add the crushed anchovies and keep warm.

Cook the pasta in a large pan of lightly salted boiling water. Drain when just *al dente* and combine with the sauce, to which the chopped parsley has been added at the last moment. Stir well then transfer to a baking dish. Lightly brown the breadcrumbs in oil, then sprinkle over the dish. Place in the oven for a few minutes until nicely browned. Serve hot.

BUCATINI ALLA MARINARA
FISHERMAN-STYLE BUCATINI

Difficulty 2

Ingredients for 4 people
Preparation time: 35' (preparation: 15' – cooking: 20')

14 oz (400 g) bucatini
5 oz (150 g) calamari
10 oz (300 g) mussels
10 oz (300 g) clams
5 oz (150 g) crayfish
1 clove garlic
¼ cup (60 ml) extra virgin olive oil
1 tbs chopped parsley
1 sage leaf
4 oz (100 g) tomato pulp (passata)
½ cup (100 ml) dry white wine
Salt
Pepper

Method

Clean the clams very carefully, rinsing them several times under running water.

Treat the mussels the same way, scraping them well. Place the mussels and the clams in a pan with a little oil, cover with a lid and put over a moderate heat, shaking the pan from time to time. Leave them to open, then shell and place in a terrine.

Clean the calamari and slice them. Remove the intestines from the crayfish.

Filter the liquid from the clams and the mussels and transfer it to a bowl. Put a pan onto a medium heat and when hot, add a heaped spoonful of chopped parsley, the sage leaf and, straight after, the calamari.

Fry gently for a while, add the white wine and cook until completely evaporated. Add the tomato pulp. Continue cooking for a few minutes, then pour in some of the reserved stock from the mussels and clams. Cover the pan and leave to cook for 6–8 minutes.

Add the mussels, clams, and crayfish. Cook the pasta *al dente* in a large pan of lightly salted boiling water. Drain and coat with the prepared sauce. Sprinkle over the parsley and some ground pepper before serving.

BUCATINI CON MOLLICA DI PANE
BUCATINI WITH BREADCRUMBS

Difficulty 1

Ingredients for 4 people
Preparation time: 25' (preparation: 10' – cooking: 15')

14 oz (400 g) bucatini
4 anchovies
4 tbs breadcrumbs
¼ cup (60 ml) extra virgin olive oil
1 pinch hot chili powder
Salt

Method

Bone and clean the anchovies. Heat half the oil in a skillet over a medium heat and add the anchovies.

Fry gently and break up the fish. In another skillet toast the breadcrumbs on a medium heat and season with the chilli powder.

Cook the pasta in a large pan of lightly salted boiling water and drain when *al dente*. Dress with the anchovies and the toasted breadcrumbs.

CALAMARI CON COZZE E VONGOLE
CALAMARI WITH MUSSELS AND CLAMS

Difficulty 1

Ingredients for 4 people
Preparation time: 30' (preparation: 15' – cooking: 15')

14 oz (400 g) calamari
7 oz (200 g) clams
7 oz (200 g) mussels
⅓ cup (80 ml) extra virgin olive oil
2 cloves garlic
2 dried chillies
14 oz (400 g) tomatoes
1 tbs chopped parsley
5 leaves basil
Salt
Pepper

Method

Heat ¼ cup (60 ml) of oil in a skillet over a moderate heat. Crush the garlic and add half. Crumble in the chillies, add the mussels and clams. Cover and leave the shellfish to open.

When somewhat cooled, shell the mussels and clams, reserving all the cooking liquid. Keep everything warm. Cut the tomatoes into cubes. Heat the remaining oil in another skillet over a medium heat, add the remaining garlic and the tomatoes. Cook for 10 minutes; add the mussels, the clams, and the reserved liquid, and cook for a further 5 minutes. Season with salt and pepper to taste, add the chopped parsley and the basil leaves torn up roughly by hand.

Cook the pasta in a large pan of lightly salted boiling water. Drain when *al dente* and dress with the prepared sauce. Serve immediately.

CASARECCE SICILIANE CON FINOCCHI, CAROTE E CIPOLLE
SICILIAN CASARECCE WITH BRAISED FENNEL, CARROTS AND SPRING ONIONS

Difficulty 1

Ingredients for 4 people
Preparation time: 30' (preparation: 5' – cooking: 25')

14 oz (400 g) casarecce
9 oz (250 g) fennel
4 oz (100 g) carrot
7 oz (200 g) spring onion
2 cloves garlic
3 oz (80 g) grated Parmigiano
1 tbs chopped feathery fennel leaves
1¾ cup (400 ml) extra virgin olive oil
Salt

Method

Cut the fennel bulbs in half, then into thin slices. Scrape the carrot and cut into rounds about ⅛ in (3 mm) thick.

Chop the garlic. Slice the onions into strips about ½ in (1 cm) wide.

Heat the oil in a large skillet on a medium heat, and add the garlic, fennel and carrot.

Cook the ingredients, covered, for about 10 minutes over a medium heat. Season with salt and black pepper, stirring from time to time. Add the onion to the mixture and cook for a further 3 minutes.

Cook the pasta in a large pan of lightly salted boiling water. Drain when *al dente* and dress with the sauce.

As a final touch, sprinkle over the chopped fennel leaves and the Parmigiano.

CASTELLANE CON CALAMARETTI
CASTELLANE WITH BABY SQUID

Difficulty 1

Ingredients for 4 people
Preparation time: 25' (preparation: 15' – cooking: 10')

14 oz (400 g) castellane
10 oz (300 g) cleaned calamari
¼ cup (50 ml) verdicchio wine
2 spoonfuls chopped parsley
1 clove garlic
2 tbs (40 ml) extra virgin olive oil
1 dried chilli
Salt

Method

Heat the oil in a large skillet over a medium heat. Slice the calamari. Add the garlic and the calamari. Cook for 5 minutes, add the wine, and leave to evaporate completely. Season to taste and add the chopped parsley.

Cook the pasta in a large pan of lightly salted boiling water. Drain when *al dente*. Transfer the pasta into the pan in which the sauce has been cooked. Serve immediately.

Italian Region: Marche.

CAVATELLI CON POMODORO E RICOTTA MARZOTICA
CAVATELLI WITH TOMATO AND RICOTTA MARZOTICA

Difficulty 1

Ingredients for 4 people
Preparation time: 25' (preparation: 15' – cooking: 10')

14 oz (400 g) cavatelli
14 oz (400 g) tomatoes
3 oz (80 g) ricotta
2 tbs (40 ml) extra virgin olive oil
2½ oz (60 g) carrot
2½ oz (60 g) onion
2½ oz (60 g) celery
4 basil leaves
Salt
Pepper

Method

Wash and chop the tomatoes.
Trim or peel and chop all the vegetables. Place a pan onto a medium heat, add the tomatoes and the other vegetables, and cook for 10–15 minutes.

Remove the vegetables. Liquidize the tomatoes in a food processor and place the pulp into a pan; add the oil and season with salt.

Place over a medium heat and bring to the boil.

Cook the pasta in a pan of lightly salted boiling water. Remove and drain a couple of minutes before it is cooked and transfer it to the pan with the tomatoes. Continue cooking the pasta in the sauce for a further 2 minutes on a high heat.

Add two thirds of the ricotta, stir well, and serve onto the plates. Garnish each plate with a basil leaf and dot over the remaining ricotta.

CELLENTANI AL SUGO DI VERDURE
CELLENTANI WITH VEGETABLE SAUCE

Difficulty 1

Ingredients for 4 people
Preparation time: 30' (preparation: 10' – cooking: 20')

14 oz (400 g) cellentani
¼ cup (50 ml) extra virgin olive oil
1 small leek
1 stick celery
1 small carrot
1 zucchino (courgette)
2 oz (50 g) peas
1 lb 2 oz (500 g) tomato pulp/passata
6 basil leaves
½ cup (100 ml) vegetable stock
Salt
Pepper

Method

If using canned peas, drain them. If using frozen or fresh peas, briefly blanch them in salted water. Clean the rest of the vegetables and dice them quite small.

Place a pan onto a medium heat with the oil and add the vegetables. Cook for a couple of minutes until golden brown and then pour in the hot stock. Continue cooking for another 5 minutes and stir in the tomato pulp. Cook for a further 10 minutes or so on a high heat and season to taste. Place the pasta in a pan of lightly salted boiling water and drain when *al dente*.

Coat with the sauce and garnish with basil leaves that have been torn by hand. Serve straightaway.

CELLENTANI AL TONNO
CELLENTANI WITH TUNA

Difficulty 1

Ingredients for 4 people
Preparation time: 25' (preparation: 10' – cooking: 15')

14 oz (400 g) cellentani
3 anchovies
4 oz (100 g) canned tuna
¼ cup (60 ml) extra virgin olive oil
1 clove garlic
1 lb 2oz (500 g) tomatoes
1 tbs chopped oregano
Salt
Pepper

Method

Put the oil in a skillet and add the garlic, but remove when the oil heats up. Cut the anchovy fillets into small pieces and add. Skin, deseed, and chop the tomatoes. Add to the skillet after about 2 minutes. Cook for about 8 minutes.

Flake the tuna with a fork and add to the pan with the oregano and ground pepper. Adjust the salt to taste and cook for a further 2 minutes. Cook the pasta in a pan of lightly salted boiling water. Drain when *al dente*.

Dress with the sauce and serve.

DITALI CON ZUCCHINE E RICOTTA
DITALI WITH ZUCCHINI AND RICOTTA

Difficulty 1

Ingredients for 4 people
Preparation time: 37' (preparation: 25' – cooking: 12')

14 oz (400 g) ditali
12 oz (350 g) zucchini (courgettes)
4 oz (100 g) ricotta
2 oz (50 g) onion
2 oz (50 g) grated Parmigiano
¼ cup (60 ml) extra virgin olive oil
Salt
Pepper

Method

Chop the onion. Wash and slice the zucchini (courgettes). Place a pan onto a medium heat. Add a little oil and cook the onion lightly until it softens. Add the zucchini, season to taste with salt and pepper, and cover.

After 15 minutes or so, remove the lid and allow the zucchini to brown lightly. Cook until all the liquid has evaporated.

Place the pasta in plenty of lightly salted boiling water. Drain when *al dente*. Transfer to a bowl and dress with the zucchini and the ricotta, lightly mashed with a fork, stirring well. Sprinkle with Parmigiano and serve hot.

Italian Region: Campania.

ELICHE BOTTARGA, AGLIO E PEPERONCINO
ELICHE WITH FISH ROE, GARLIC, AND CHILI

Difficulty 1

Ingredients for 4 people
Preparation time: 15' (preparation: 5' – cooking: 10')

14 oz (400 g) eliche
¼ cup (60 ml) extra virgin olive oil
3 oz (80 g) fish roe
1 clove garlic
1 dried chilli
Salt

Method

Finely chop the garlic; grind the chilli. Heat the oil in a skillet over a low heat, add the garlic and the chilli. Fry gently for a couple of minutes.

Cook the pasta in a pan of lightly salted boiling water. Drain when *al dente*. Coat with the sauce. Garnish with the fish roe and serve.

In Italy bottarga, or cured fish roe (the dried egg-laden ovarian sac of, usually, mullet or tuna), is considered the poor man's caviar. The main areas of production are Tuscany, Sardinia, and Sicily. It is sold commercially in powder form or can be found whole.

FARFALLE FANTASIA
FARFALLE WITH PROSCIUTTO AND OLIVES

Difficulty 1

Ingredients for 4 people
Preparation time: 25' (preparation: 10' – cooking: 15')

14 oz (400 g) farfalle
¼ oz (10 g) butter
4 oz (100 g) thickly sliced prosciutto
10 pitted black olives
¼ cup (50 ml) white wine
⅔ cup (150 ml) cream
1 cup (250 ml) tomato sauce
1 dessertspoon finely chopped fresh oregano
Salt
Pepper

Method

Dice the prosciutto and roughly chop the olives. Heat the butter in a large skillet over a low heat and gently fry the prosciutto and the olives for 2 minutes or so. Turn the heat up, add wine to cover, and cook until the liquid has completely evaporated. Add the cream and the tomato sauce and cook for about 10 minutes. Season with salt and pepper to taste.

Cook the pasta in a pan of lightly salted boiling water and drain when *al dente*. Dress with the prepared sauce, sprinkle with fresh oregano, and serve.

FARFALLE CON CAPPERI, TONNO E MENTA
FARFALLE WITH CAPERS, TUNA, AND MINT

Difficulty 1

Ingredients for 4 people
Preparation time: 15' (preparation: 5' – cooking: 10')

14 oz (400 g) farfalle
4 oz (100 g) capers in brine
1 small bunch mint
7 oz (200 g) canned tuna
2 tbs (40 ml) extra virgin olive oil
Salt
Pepper

Method

Rinse the capers under running water. Chop the capers and the mint and combine with the drained tuna. Place the mixture in a bowl with the extra virgin olive oil. Season with pepper.

Cook the pasta in a pan of lightly salted boiling water and drain when *al dente*.

Coat with the prepared sauce and serve immediately.

Italian Region: Sicily.

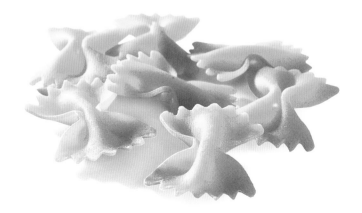

FIOCCHI RIGATI AL TONNO FRESCO
FIOCCHI RIGATI WITH TUNA

Difficulty 1

Ingredients for 4 people
Preparation time: 25' (preparation: 10' – cooking: 15')

14 oz (400 g) fiocchi rigati
¼ cup (50 ml) extra virgin olive oil
9 oz (250 g) fresh tuna
10 oz (300 g) tomato sauce
2 tbs chopped parsley
Salt
Pepper

Method

Heat the oil in a skillet over a high heat and fry the fresh tuna until it takes
on a golden color. Drain, sprinkle with salt to taste, and cut into cubes.
Place another skillet onto a low heat with the tomato sauce.
When hot, add the fried tuna and the chopped parsley.

Cook for about 10 minutes; adjust the seasoning. Cook the pasta in a pan
of lightly salted boiling water and drain when *al dente*. Dress with the
prepared sauce and serve.

Italian Region: Sicily.

FOOD HISTORY

*Tuna is one of the most characteristic fish of the Mediterranean. Fished for thousands of
years, the methods for catching the fish have developed over the centuries. Now no longer
used, the traditional tonnare, or large tuna fishing nets can, however, still be seen almost
everywhere: in restaurants, tourist attractions and museums.*
*In Sicily, however, two tuna hunts still take place near Trapani: one in Bonagia and the other
in Favignana.*
*Here, you can witness the mattanza, the ancient passage of the large tuna from the Atlantic
to the Mediterranean at the end of spring. Over 660 lb (300 kg) of fish are caught in large
nets attached to boats with outboard motors. The chief, or rais, sings traditional Sicilian
songs as he gives the fishermen orders. A relic from an older world, the tuna hunts are
almost impossible to understand. They are a combination of tradition and superstition,
a fight for survival, and a desire for wealth. A tragic, one-of-a-kind show.*

FUSILLI BUCATI CORTI ALLA CRUDAIOLA
FUSILLI WITH UNCOOKED SAUCE

Difficulty 1

Ingredients for 4 people
Preparation time: 20' (preparation: 10' – cooking: 10')

14 oz (400 g) fusilli bucati corti
¼ cup (50 ml) extra virgin olive oil
1 lb 2 oz (500 g) tomatoes
10 basil leaves
1 clove garlic
Salt
Pepper

Method

Wash the tomatoes, remove the seeds, and slice thinly. Finely chop the garlic; tear the basil leaves. Place into a large bowl with the oil, the basil leaves, garlic, salt, and pepper.

Boil the spaghetti in lightly salted water and drain when *al dente*.
Add the pasta to the bowl, toss well in the sauce, and serve.

FUSILLI CON TONNO, OLIVE E CAPPERI
FUSILLI WITH TUNA, OLIVES, AND CAPERS

Difficulty 1

Ingredients for 4 people
Preparation time: 50' (preparation: 40' – cooking: 10')

14 oz (400 g) fusilli
5 oz (150 g) cherry tomatoes
5 oz (150 g) black olives
4 oz (100 g) drained tuna
2½ oz (60 g) cubed mozzarella cheese
¾ oz (20 g) capers
1 tbs chopped basil
¼ cup (50 ml) extra virgin olive oil
3 tbs lemon juice
Salt
Pepper

Method

Cook the pasta, drain when *al dente*, then drizzle over a small amount of olive oil. Leave to cool, cover with plastic wrap, and chill in the refrigerator.

Halve or quarter the cherry tomatoes, depending on their size. In a bowl, combine the tomatoes, olives, tuna, mozzarella, capers, and basil.
Add with the remaining oil and adjust the seasoning.

Dress the pasta with the prepared sauce, finally adding the lemon juice.

Leave to rest for half an hour before serving.

GEMELLI CON SALSICCIA E PORRI
GEMELLI WITH ITALIAN SAUSAGE AND LEEKS

Difficulty 1

Ingredients for 4 people
Preparation time: 25' (preparation: 15' – cooking: 10')

14 oz (400 g) gemelli
14 oz (400 g) pork sausage
4 oz (100 g) leek
¾ oz (20 g) extra virgin olive oil
½ cup (100 ml) white wine

½ oz (15 g) butter
1½ oz (40 g) grated Parmigiano
2 tbs chopped parsley
Salt
Black pepper

Method

Slice the leeks thinly and clean by rinsing them well in water to remove any soil.
Remove the skin from the sausages.
Heat the oil in a skillet over a high heat, add the sausages, and cook until they have browned. Add the leek, cook for three minutes, and pour in the white wine to cover. Continue cooking until the liquid has reduced by half. Adjust the seasoning.

Cook the pasta in a pan of lightly salted boiling water and drain when *al dente*. Dress with the prepared sauce and the butter, stirring well. Sprinkle grated Parmigiano over the pasta and garnish with parsley before serving.

FOOD HISTORY

The leek is a close relative of the onion, but it has a more delicate flavor. Leeks are one of the few ingredients that were considered a fundamental source of nutrition during periods of famine in the Middle Ages. Leeks have been eaten since ancient times: Although we do not know the exact date when they were discovered, there is no doubt that they were already cultivated 4,000 years ago on the banks of the Nile, as illustrated in the hieroglyphics inside the pyramids. Even the workers who built the huge buildings ate, among other things, leeks and onions.
From the Nile Valley, leeks spread all around the Mediterranean, becoming extremely popular in ancient Rome, where the Roman Emperor Nero was given the nickname "il porrofago" (or leek eater) for his habit of eating a lot of leeks to clear his voice.
According to an ancient legend, on the eve of a battle against the Saxons, Saint David advised the Welsh to wear leeks on their hats to distinguish them from their enemies. After a great victory, leeks became one of the symbols of the Welsh, who wear hats with leeks on Saint David's Day.
Leeks and sausage are some of the most typical ingredients in simple home cooking and they make this Italian first course very substantial and tasty.

GNOCCHI DI SEMOLA CON I BROCCOLI
SEMOLINA GNOCCHI WITH BROCCOLI

Difficulty 1

Ingredients for 4 people
Preparation time: 28' (preparation: 20' – cooking: 8')

14 oz (400 g) semolina gnocchi
14 oz (400 g) broccoli
2 tbs (30 ml) olive oil
2 cloves garlic
2 oz (50 g) grated Pecorino
2 oz (50 g) grated young Caciocavallo
2 oz (50 g) grated mature Caciocavallo
Salt

Method

Wash the broccoli and separate into florets, then steam it in a pasta colander placed over a pan of water. As soon as it is cooked, drain and set aside. Chop the garlic. Heat the oil in a large skillet over a medium heat, add the garlic and the broccoli. Season and cook for 2 minutes.
Cook the gnocchi in a pan of lightly salted boiling water and drain when *al dente*.
Dress with the prepared sauce.
Finally add the three grated cheeses.

There are a number of variations on this recipe: the following one is from Enna.
Cook 1 lb 2oz (500 g) of broccoli, drain, and cut up into pieces. Gently fry in a skillet together with half a glass of olive oil and two finely chopped cloves of garlic. Prepare two cups of tomato sauce. Cook 14 oz (400 g) of spaghetti in the water that the broccoli was boiled in; drain and dress with the tomato sauce, the sautéed broccoli, and plenty of grated Pecorino.

Italian Region: Sicily.

INSALATA DI CONCHIGLIE CON ASPARAGI
CONCHIGLIE PASTA SALAD WITH ASPARAGUS

Difficulty 1

Ingredients for 4 people
Preparation time: 10' (preparation: 10' – cooking: 15')

14 oz (400 g) conchiglie
5 oz (150 g) white asparagus
5 oz (150 g) cherry tomatoes
4 oz (100 g) mozzarella
4 tsp (20 ml) balsamic vinegar
2 tsp (10 ml) white wine vinegar
2 sprigs fresh oregano
¼ cup (50 ml) extra virgin olive oil
Salt
Pepper

Method

Cook the pasta in a pan of lightly salted boiling water. Drain when *al dente*. Transfer to a dish, add a little oil, and leave to cool.

Wash the tomatoes and cut them into segments or in half, depending on their size.

Clean the asparagus, removing the tough white part and cut into small pieces, then cook in boiling water until *al dente*. Drain and prevent further cooking by plunging briefly into cold water, then drain again.

Prepare a simple dressing by beating the oil and the balsamic and wine vinegars together, adding salt, pepper, and oregano leaves. In a salad bowl combine the pasta with the asparagus, the cubed mozzarella, and the chopped tomatoes. Dress with the sauce, stir carefully, and serve.

INSALATA DI FUSILLI CON VERDURE E CALAMARI
FUSILLI SALAD WITH VEGETABLES AND CALAMARI

Difficulty 1

Ingredients for 4 people
Preparation time: 25' (preparation: 15' – cooking: 10')

14 oz (400 g) fusilli
2 carrots
2 zucchini (courgettes)
2 artichokes
3 calamari (squid)

1 bouquet garni
¼ cup (60 ml) extra virgin olive oil
Juice of 1 lemon
Salt
White pepper

Method

Wash and peel the carrots. Wash and dry the zucchini (courgettes).
Remove the tough outer leaves from the artichokes. Halve them lengthwise and scrape out the "hay" in the center. Cut them into thin strips and place in a bowl of water with the juice of half a lemon to prevent them turning black. Cut the carrots and the zucchini into thin strips.

Clean the squid by removing the skin from the sac and separating the tentacles from the body. Discard the entrails and the transparent cartilage. Remove the beak located in the center of the tentacles and also the eyes. Cut the flesh into very thin strips.

Cook the pasta in a pan of lightly salted boiling water. 5 minutes before the end of cooking, add the vegetables to the water in the pan. Stir and cook for 1 minute, then add the calamari and cook for 2 more minutes. Drain when the pasta is *al dente*. Transfer to a dish and allow to cool, adding a little light dressing of oil. When quite cold, dress with the rest of the oil and lemon juice. Adjust the seasoning to taste and serve over a bed of lettuce.

FOOD HISTORY

Artichokes are a typical Mediterranean plant and were already known and eaten by the ancient Egyptians. The ancient Greeks, however, believed they had a very interesting origin. Legend has it that Zeus, the father of all the gods, fell in love with an extremely beautiful woman by the name of Cynara due to her ash- (cenere in Italian) blond hair. Zeus seduced the woman and brought her up to Mount Olympus. The young lady, however, quickly began to miss her mother and without telling Zeus, decided to return to the world of the mortals, to be with her. When the god discovered that she had escaped, he went down to earth in fury and punished her by turning her into a spiny plant. The plant came to be known by the name Cynara, or carciofo (Italian for artichoke).
The first "artichoke queen," elected each year in Castroville, California, during the annual Artichoke Festival, was Marilyn Monroe. She was crowned queen in 1949.
This fresh and light pasta salad is an ideal way to enjoy typical Italian flavors on a hot summer day.

INSALATA DI PENNE ALLA NAPOLETANA
NEAPOLITAN PENNE SALAD

Difficulty 1

Ingredients for 4 people
Preparation time: 15' (preparation: 6' – cooking: 9')

14 oz (400 g) penne
9 oz (250 g) plum tomatoes
5 oz (150 g) buffalo mozzarella
2 fillets salted anchovies
2 tbs (30 ml) extra virgin olive oil
4 leaves basil
Salt
Pepper

Method

Thinly slice the mozzarella; chop the anchovies, tomatoes, and basil leaves. Place everything in a salad bowl, then add the oil and season with salt and pepper.

Cook the pasta in a pan of lightly salted boiling water. Drain when *al dente* and transfer to the salad bowl. Stir well to combine and serve at once.

Italian Region: Campania.

LA PASTA DEL CATTIVO TEMPO
BAD-WEATHER PASTA

Difficulty 1

Ingredients for 4 people
Preparation time: 52' (preparation: 40' – cooking: 12')

14 oz (400 g) ditalini rigati
9 oz (250 g) broccoli
2 tbs (40 ml) extra virgin olive oil
1 tbs chopped parsley
1 clove crushed garlic
Black or red pepper

12 desalted anchovies
4 tsp (20 ml) dry white wine
4 tbs breadcrumbs
12 chopped black olives
Salt

Method

Clean the broccoli and cook in a pan of lightly salted boiling water.
Bone and clean the anchovies.
Heat the oil in a skillet over a low heat. Add the garlic and fry gently until it just starts to color – after about a minute. Add the parsley and the anchovies, crushing them with a wooden spoon. Add the white wine to cover and simmer until it has evaporated.
Add the broccoli, making sure that it does not overcook.
Put a small pan onto a low heat and dry-toast the breadcrumbs; add the olives.
Cook the pasta in a pan of lightly salted boiling water. Drain when *al dente* and toss the pasta with the prepared sauce.
Sprinkle over the toasted breadcrumbs and chopped olives and serve.

Italian Region: Sicily.

LINGUINE AL CARTOCCIO
LINGUINE IN FOIL

Difficulty 2

Ingredients for 4 people
Preparation time: 35' (preparation: 20' – cooking: 15')

14 oz (400 g) linguine
7 oz (200 g) sliced calamari
4 oz (100 g) shrimps
4 oz (100 g) cleaned mussels
7 oz (200 g) tomato sauce
1 tbs chopped parsley
¼ cup (50 ml) extra virgin olive oil
1 clove garlic
Salt

Method

Heat the oil in a skillet over a medium heat, add the garlic and gently fry. Add the shellfish, the parsley and the tomato sauce, and simmer for 10 minutes.

Cook the linguine in a pan of slightly salted boiling water and drain when *al dente*. Toss the pasta with the seafood sauce and transfer onto aluminum foil. Wrap as a parcel and cook in a hot oven at 400°F (200°C) for about five minutes. Serve immediately.

Italian Region: Apulia.

LINGUINE ALL'ARAGOSTA
LINGUINE WITH LOBSTER

Difficulty 1

Ingredients for 4 people
Preparation time: 30' (preparation: 20' – cooking: 10')

14 oz (400 g) linguine
7 oz (200 g) lobster flesh in pieces
1¼ oz (30 g) butter
5 oz (150 g) fresh cream
1 tbs concentrated tomato paste
½ cup (100 ml) brandy
½ small onion
Salt
Pepper

Method

Finely chop the onion. In a large skillet, fry the onion in the butter until
it starts to color. Stir in the lobster and allow the flavors to develop, then
pour over the brandy and cook until it has evaporated. Add salt, pepper,
the tomato paste, and the cream, and simmer for a few minutes.
Cook the pasta in a large pan of lightly salted boiling water. Drain when
al dente and toss in the prepared sauce.

Italian Region: Campania.

MACCHERONCINI CON POLPETTINE DI CARNE
MACCHERONCINI WITH MEATBALLS

Difficulty 2

Ingredients for 4 people
Preparation time: 1 h 5' (preparation: 40' – cooking: 25')

14 oz (400 g) maccheroncini
9 oz (250 g) beef tenderloin
2 oz (50 g) prosciutto
½ onion
¼ cup (50 ml) extra virgin olive oil
1¼ oz (30 g) butter
1 cup (200 ml) white wine
12 oz (350 g) tomato pulp/passata
2 oz (50 g) grated Parmigiano

FOR THE MEAT BALLS
1¼ oz (30 g) beef bone marrow
2 oz (50 g) breadcrumbs
2 tbs (30 ml) milk
1 clove garlic
1 tbs chopped parsley
50 g flour
2 egg yolks
1 zest of lemon
Salt
Pepper

Method

Chop the onion and the prosciutto. Heat the oil in a skillet over a medium heat. Add the onion and the prosciutto. As soon as they start to color, add the meat and brown slowly. Pour over the wine and cook until it has evaporated. Add the tomato pulp and 1½ cups (300 ml) of water to cover the meat. Cook covered over a low heat for about 2 hours.
When the meat is cooked, remove and leave to cool. Press the sauce through a fine sieve and return it to the pan.

Soak the breadcrumbs in milk, then squeeze out to remove the excess liquid. In a food processor, mix the meat, the beef marrow, garlic, parsley, and breadcrumbs. Transfer the mixture to a bowl.

Finish with a little grated lemon zest and a pinch of salt and pepper. Stir in the two yolks, combining all the ingredients well. With the palms of your hands form small balls. Dip these in flour and cook in a small amount of lightly salted boiling water. Keep the meatballs warm in their cooking water on the edge of the stove.

Cook the maccheroncini in a large pan of lightly salted boiling water. Drain when *al dente* and transfer to a preheated serving dish. Dot with butter and sprinkle over the grated Parmigiano. Cover with half the sauce and arrange the meatballs on top. Combine and serve with the rest of the sauce.

MACCHERONCINI IN PASTICCIO
MACCHERONCINI PIE

Difficulty 2

Ingredients for 4 people
Preparation time: 1 h 40' (preparation: 1 h – cooking: 40')

9 oz (250 g) maccheroncini
1 oz (20 g) butter to grease the pie dish

FOR THE SHORT CRUST PASTRY
9 oz (250 g) flour
4½ oz (125 g) sugar
4½ oz (125 g) lard
3 egg yolks

FOR THE SAUCE
3 oz (80 g) grated Parmigiano
½ cup (100 ml) meat sauce (ragù)
4 oz (100 g) mozzarella
1 cup (200 ml) béchamel sauce
7 oz (200 g) ground pork
4 oz (100 g) chicken liver
½ cup (100 ml) red wine
2 tbs (40 ml) extra virgin olive oil
7 oz (200 g) tomato pulp/passata
1 onion
Salt

Method

Prepare short crust pastry with the flour, sugar, lard, and egg yolks. Leave to rest for about 30 minutes.
Cook the pasta in a pan of boiling water. Drain when *al dente* and dress with the Parmigiano and meat sauce; leave to cool.
Grind the chicken livers. Heat a little oil in a small skillet over a medium heat. Add the onion and cook until soft. Then add the ground meat and the chicken livers, and brown. Pour over the red wine and cook until evaporated. Add the tomato pulp (passata), season, and cook for 30 minutes. Butter a 6¼-cup (1½-l) pie dish.
Roll out the pastry to a thickness of ¼ in (5 mm). Cut out a circle the same size as the bottom of the dish and a rectangular strip that is wide enough and long enough to line the inside of the dish comfortably. Using your fingers, lightly press the join between the bottom and side together to make a good seal. Turn half of the maccheroncini into the pie dish, hollowing out the centre slightly. Cut the mozzarella in cubes.
Place the prepared ragù into this hollow and add the mozzarella. Fill with the remaining maccheroncini; place another disc of the short crust pastry on top to cover. Seal as before. Bake the pie in the oven at 360°F (180°C) for about 40 minutes or until the pastry is cooked and golden. Remove from the oven, leave to rest for 5–6 minutes and then turn out the pie onto a serving dish.

MACCHERONI E RICOTTA IN TIMBALLO
MACARONI AND RICOTTA PIE

Difficulty 2

Ingredients for 4 people
Preparation time: 1 h 20' (preparation: 40' – cooking: 40')

14 oz (400 g) macaroni
10 oz (300 g) ground meat
1 small onion
1 stick celery
1 small carrot
¼ cup (60 ml) extra virgin olive oil
1 cup (200 ml) red wine
7 oz (200 g) canned tomatoes
7 oz (200 g) ricotta
4 oz (100 g) caciotta cheese
2 oz (50 g) grated Parmigiano
Salt

Method

Finely chop the onion, celery, and carrot. Place a pan on the stove and add the ground meat and the chopped vegetables. Coat with the oil. Slowly brown the meat and soften the vegetables. When these are well cooked and the meat is a nice brown color, season with a little salt. Add the red wine, a little at a time, and simmer until it has evaporated. Add the tomato sauce with enough water to cover; simmer gently.
When the meat is well cooked, the sauce will be considerably reduced. Skim the fat from the surface with a spoon. Grind the meat. Set the sauce to one side.
Place the ricotta in a bowl and stir in a few spoonfuls of warm water until it has a creamy consistency. Add the ground meat and the caciotta cut into little cubes.
Cook the pasta in a pan of lightly salted boiling water. Drain when *al dente*, coat with the prepared sauce, and sprinkle with the Parmigiano.
In an ovenproof dish, alternate layers of the dressed macaroni and the meat sauce. Pour the remainder of the sauce over the top and place the pie in the oven to heat through for about 10 minutes. Transfer to a serving dish.

MACCHERONI GRATINATI
MACARONI BAKE

Difficulty 2

Ingredients for 4 people
Preparation time: 35' (preparation: 5' – cooking: 30')

14 oz (400 g) macaroni
5 oz (150 g) butter
5 oz (150 g) grated Parmigiano
2½ oz (60 g) flour
3¼ cups (750 ml) milk
1¼ oz (30 g) breadcrumbs
Nutmeg

Method

Melt 2 oz (50 g) of butter in a casserole and add the flour, a little at a time. Stir in the milk with the help of a whisk. Cook over a low heat, bringing it to the boil slowly. Season with a pinch of salt and nutmeg.

Cook the macaroni in a large pan of lightly salted boiling water. Drain when *al dente* and place in a large dish. Add 2 oz (50 g) of butter, the prepared béchamel sauce (reserving a small amount) and a couple of spoonfuls of grated Parmigiano. Stir all the ingredients together well to combine.

Grease an ovenproof dish with ¾ oz (20 g) of butter, add the macaroni, and top with the rest of the béchamel sauce. Sprinkle over the breadcrumbs mixed with the same quantity of grated Parmigiano. Dot with the rest of the butter and place in the oven at 360°F (180°C) for around 20 minutes. Remove from the oven and serve as soon as it has turned golden brown.

MAFALDINE ALLA NAPOLETANA
NEAPOLITAN MAFALDINE

Difficulty 1

Ingredients for 4 people
Preparation time: 25' (preparation: 10' – cooking: 15')

14 oz (400 g) mafaldine
2 oz (50 g) lard
14 oz (400 g) peeled tomatoes
2½ oz (60 g) grated Pecorino
Salt
Pepper

Method

Put a pan over a moderate heat, add the lard, and when it has melted, add the peeled tomatoes. Cook for 15 minutes; season to taste with salt and pepper.

Cook the pasta in a pan of lightly salted boiling water. Dress with the prepared sauce, sprinkle over the grated Pecorino, and serve.

Italian Region: Campania.

MALLOREDDUS AL TONNO CON BOTTARGA DI MUGGINE
MALLOREDDUS WITH TUNA AND FISH ROE

Difficulty 2

Ingredients for 4 people
Preparation time: 30' (preparation: 25' – cooking: 5')

14 oz (400 g) malloreddus
7 oz (200 g) fresh tuna
4½ oz (120 g) onion
¼ cup (50 ml) extra virgin olive oil
½ oz (15 g) capers
4 oz (100 g) fresh tomatoes
1¼ oz (30 g) wild fennel
½ cup (100 ml) white wine
¾ oz (20 g) mullet fish roe
¼ oz (10 g) fish stock (optional)
Salt
Pepper

Method

Cut the onion into thin strips and dice the tuna. Heat the oil in a large skillet over a medium heat; add the onion and the tuna. Cook for a couple of minutes until brown, and then add the capers.

Cover with the white wine and cook until it has evaporated. Season to taste. If necessary, add some fish stock to the tuna. Roughly chop the tomatoes and half of the fennel; stir in.

If the sauce becomes too dry add a little of the fish stock.

Cook the pasta in a pan of lightly salted water. Drain when *al dente*. Coat with the sauce. Add the wild fennel and sprinkle the fish roe over the top.

Chef's Tips

The malloreddus must be well cooked (they take a particularly long time to cook) and stirred frequently as they tend to stick to one another during cooking. The bottarga is always added at the end of cooking, away from the heat, in order to avoid losing its fragrance.

Malloreddus are little gnocchi (gnochetti), typical of Sardinia, usually made from durum wheat that is simply mixed with water. Served as a first course, they can be accompanied by various sauces, depending on their shape. In Sardinia, they are known by the name of "aidos cicones" or "maccarones cravaos."

Italian Region: Sardinia.

MEZZANI CON LE SARDE ALLA SICILIANA

MEZZANI WITH SARDINES ALLA SICILIANA

Difficulty 1

Ingredients for 4 people
Preparation time: 45' (preparation: 15' – cooking: 30')

14 oz (400 g) mezzani
7 oz (200 g) sardines
¼ cup (50 ml) extra virgin olive oil
2 fronds wild fennel
3 cloves garlic
1 chopped onion
3 oz (80 g) desalted anchovies
1¼ oz (30 g) seedless sultana grapes
1¼ oz (30 g) pine nuts
1 tsp chopped parsley
1 pinch saffron
Salt
Pepper

Method

Dissolve the saffron in a few drops of water. Heat 4 tsp oil in a large skillet, add 2 cloves of garlic, a few spoonfuls of cold water, and a pinch of saffron. Season with salt and pepper, and cook for about 4 minutes. Bone and wash the sardines, then add them and continue to cook for a few more minutes. Remove the garlic, and reserve the sardines.

To prepare the sauce, sauté gently one clove of garlic in a few spoonfuls of oil with the chopped onion until it starts to color. Blanch and chop the wild fennel. Pulp the anchovy fillets in a mortar with the parsley. Add the fennel, the grapes, the pine nuts, the anchovy pulp. Dilute with a ladle of the fennel-cooking water; cook the mixture on a moderate heat for a bit longer.

In a pan, bring the fennel-cooking water to the boil, lightly salt it, and cook the pasta. Drain the mezzani when *al dente* and alternate in an ovenproof dish with layers of the sauce and the sardines, finishing with a layer of sauce. Place in a moderate oven, and bake for around 20 minutes. Serve.

Italian Region: Sicily.

MEZZE MANICHE CON FRUTTI DI MARE
MEZZE MANICHE WITH SEAFOOD SAUCE

Difficulty 2

Ingredients for 4 people
Preparation time: 50' (preparation: 30' – cooking: 20')

14 oz (400 g) mezze maniche
1 lb 2 oz (500 g) mussels
4 oz (100 g) baby calamari
1 lb 2 oz (500 g) clams
4 oz (100 g) baby cuttlefish
4 oz (100 g) shrimp tails
1¼ oz (30 g) concentrated tomato paste
¼ cup (50 ml) extra virgin olive oil
1 tbs chopped parsley
1 clove garlic
chilli pepper
Salt

Method

Heat the oil in a skillet over a medium heat. Add the garlic, chilli powder, parsley, and the tomato paste diluted in a little warm water. Simmer slowly and when it all begins to color, add the baby calamari and the cuttlefish.

Cook over a medium heat for a few minutes and then stir in the shrimp tails, the mussels and the clams. Season with a little salt. Cover and continue cooking until the mussels and the clams open up.

Place the mezze maniche in a large pan of lightly salted boiling water. Drain when *al dente*. Toss the pasta in the prepared sauce.

Italian Region: Abruzzo.

MEZZE PENNE CON LE ACCIUGHE
MEZZE PENNE WITH ANCHOVIES

Difficulty 1

Ingredients for 4 people
Preparation time: 20' (preparation: 10' − cooking: 10')

14 oz (400 g) mezze penne
¼ cup (50 ml) extra virgin olive oil
2½ oz (60 g) desalted anchovies, ground in a mortar
1 clove garlic
14 oz (400 g) tomato pulp
1 dried chilli
1 tbs chopped parsley
Salt

Method

Heat the oil in a large skillet over a medium heat, add the whole garlic clove and the chilli, and cook slowly until they begin to color. Remove the garlic. Add the ground anchovies and, straight after, the tomato pulp. Cook for about 8 minutes and season with salt to taste. Cook the pasta in a pan of lightly salted boiling water. Drain when *al dente*. Coat with the prepared sauce, add the chopped parsley, toss, and serve.

MEZZE PENNE CON OLIVE E CAPRINO
MEZZE PENNE WITH OLIVES AND GOAT'S CHEESE

Difficulty 1

Ingredients for 4 people
Preparation time: 15' (preparation: 5' – cooking: 10')

14 oz (400 g) mezze penne
7 oz (200 g) goat's cheese
1¼ oz (30 g) extra virgin olive oil
3 oz (80 g) pitted black olives
Salt

Method

Finely chop the olives.
Place the goat's cheese in a large bowl, add the oil, and mash to soften.
Add the chopped olives and stir well to combine.
Cook the pasta in a pan of lightly salted boiling water. Drain when *al dente*.
Dress with the goat's cheese and the olives.
Stir carefully and serve immediately.

MINESTRONE COL PESTO
MINESTRONE WITH PESTO

Difficulty 2

Ingredients for 4 people
Preparation time: 1 h 8' (preparation: 1 h – cooking: 8')

FOR THE PESTO
½ oz (15 g) basil
¼ oz (8 g) pine nuts
1-2 cloves garlic
½ cup (100 ml) extra virgin olive oil
1¼ oz (30 g) grated Parmigiano
¾ oz (20 g) grated matured Pecorino
Salt
Pepper

FOR THE MINESTRONE
3 oz (70 g) potatoes
3 oz (70 g) peas
3 oz (70 g) pumpkin
3 oz (70 g) head of cabbage
3 oz (70 g) fava beans

3 oz (70 g) zucchini (courgettes)
3 oz (70 g) french beans
3 oz (70 g) borlotti beans
3 oz (70 g) cannellini beans
1 tomato
½ oz (15 g) celery
½ oz (15 g) carrot
½ oz (15 g) onion
1 clove garlic
2 tbs (30 ml) extra virgin olive oil
5 oz (150 g) pesto
1½ oz (40 g) grated Parmigiano
5 oz (150 g) ditalini
10½ cups (2.5 l) water
1 tbs chopped parsley
Rock salt

Method

To make the pesto chop the garlic and the basil; add a pinch of salt to preserve the green color of the leaves. Place in a mortar the basil, garlic, and pine nuts. Grind the ingredients, adding a little oil, if necessary, to obtain a pesto.

Place the pesto in a bowl and stir in the other ingredients: the grated Parmigiano, the grated Pecorino, and the remaining oil. Season with salt and pepper to taste.

Wash and prepare all the vegetables.
Chop the garlic finely.
Cut up the vegetables, leaving whole the peas and the beans.
Bring the water to the boil in a large pan, add all the vegetables and the garlic, cook for a few minutes over a very high heat, then lower the heat and simmer, covered.

Stir the minestrone frequently in order to prevent the vegetables sticking to the bottom of the pan. Halfway through cooking, add the oil, the cheese, and the rock salt. Crush the potatoes and the beans roughly with a spoon to help the minestrone to thicken.

When the vegetables have more or less disintegrated and the minestrone has become thick and creamy, add the pasta and continue to cook.

Remove from the heat and stir in the pesto and the chopped parsley with a wooden spoon.
Leave to rest for about 10 minutes and serve in soup plates.

Italian Region: Liguria.

ORECCHIETTE CON BROCCOLI, POMODORINI E MANDORLE
ORECCHIETTE WITH BROCCOLI, CHERRY TOMATOES AND ALMONDS

Difficulty 1

Ingredients for 4 people
Preparation time: 35' (preparation: 20' – cooking: 15')

14 oz (400 g) orecchiette
12 oz (350 g) broccoli
3 oz (80 g) Pecorino
¾ oz (20 g) anchovies in brine
1 clove garlic
1¼ oz (30 g) extra virgin olive oil
7 oz (200 g) cherry tomatoes
1¼ oz (30 g) flaked almonds
Salt
Black pepper

Method

Chop the garlic. Drain and finely chop the anchovies.
Wash the broccoli, separating the florets, and partly cook in salted water for 3 minutes. Cut the cherry tomatoes in half.

Place a pan onto a medium heat and cook the garlic and the anchovies in the oil until they start to color. Then add the broccoli and the tomatoes and simmer gently for 5 minutes. Season with salt and pepper.
Cook the orecchiette in a pan of slightly salted boiling water. Drain when *al dente* and dress with the prepared sauce.

Serve the pasta decorated with shavings of Pecorino and flaked almonds.

Chef's Tips

The broccoli should be cooked in lightly salted boiling water just long enough so as to keep its bright green color and not break up. The orecchiette tend to stick together during cooking so it is advisable to stir continuously during the first minute.

This durum wheat pasta is typical of the Puglia region, where it is known as "strascinati" and is accompanied with rather liquid sauces as "strascinati" is very absorbent.

Italian Region: Apulia.

ORECCHIETTE CON CIME DI RAPE
ORECCHIETTE WITH TURNIP TOPS

Difficulty 1

Ingredients for 4 people
Preparation time: 35' (preparation: 20' – cooking: 15')

14 oz (400 g) orecchiette
3 lb (1.5 kg) turnip tops
30 salted anchovies
2 cloves garlic
¼ cup (60 ml) extra virgin olive oil
Salt
Chilli pepper

Method

Clean the turnips, keeping only the tenderest parts of the tops, then
thoroughly rinse in cold water. Finely chop the chilli pepper. Rinse and
bone the anchovies, then chop and grind them to a paste. Heat the oil
in a skillet over a moderate heat; add the chilli pepper and the garlic.
Sauté for a minute or so, until they start to brown, then add the anchovies.

Bring a large pan of water to the boil and then add salt; drop in the pasta
and after a few minutes, the turnip tops. Drain when *al dente* and dress
with the prepared sauce. If required, add more extra virgin olive oil.
Serve at once.

Italian Region: Apulia.

PACCHERI AI CARCIOFI
PACCHERI WITH ARTICHOKES

Difficulty 1

Ingredients for 4 people
Preparation time: 30' (preparation: 15' – cooking: 15')

14 oz (400 g) paccheri
14 oz (400 g) artichokes
2 cloves garlic
2 tsp lemon juice
3 oz (80 g) grated Pecorino
1½ oz (40 g) extra virgin olive oil
Salt
Chilli pepper

Method

Clean the artichokes, removing the tough outermost leaves. Cut in half, remove the fuzzy choke inside, and cut into slices. Heat half of the oil in a large skillet over a medium heat, and add the garlic, the artichokes, and the lemon juice. Season with salt and a pinch of chilli powder cooked.

Cook the paccheri pasta (similar to rigatoni but longer and bigger) in lightly salted boiling water. Drain when *al dente* and dress with the prepared sauce. Add the grated Pecorino and the rest of the extra virgin olive oil.

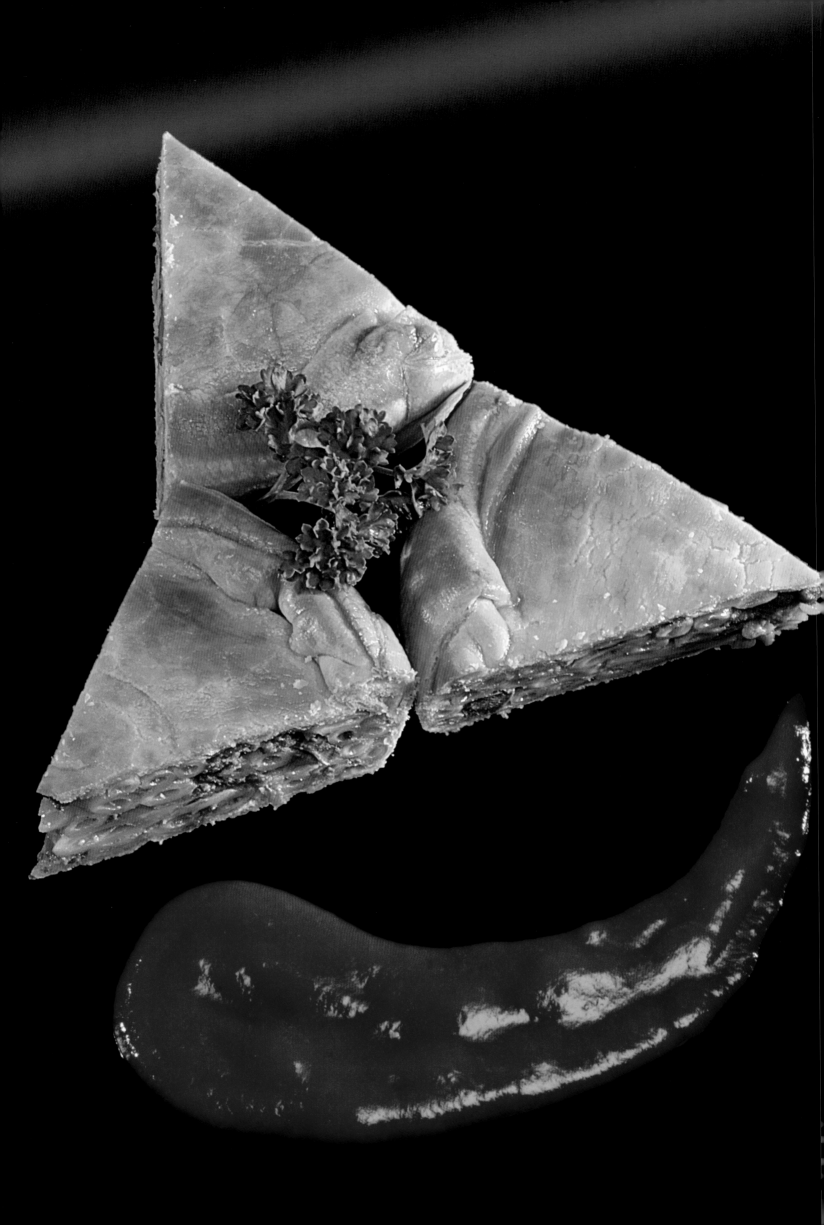

PASTICCIO DI MACCHERONI

MACARONI PIE

Difficulty 2

Ingredients for 4 people

Preparation time: 1 h 20' (preparation: 1 h – cooking: 20')

FOR THE SHORT CRUST PASTRY
1 lb (450 g) all-purpose flour
7 oz (200 g) butter
4 oz (100 g) sugar
5 egg yolks
1 tsp grated lemon zest
Salt

FOR THE RAGÙ
5 oz (150 g) ground lean veal
5 oz (150 g) ground lean beef
5 oz (150 g) ground chicken breast
5 oz (150 g) chicken giblets
¼ cup (50 ml) dry white wine

2 tsp (10 ml) marsala wine
2 oz (50 g) butter
1 stick celery
1 onion
1 carrot
¼ cup (50 ml) extra virgin olive oil
Salt
Pepper

FOR THE FILLING
2 oz (50 g) grated Parmigiano
9 oz (250 g) macaroni
1¼ lb (600 g) béchamel
Truffle

Method

Prepare the short-crust pastry. Place the flour onto the pastry board and work into a dough with the rest of the ingredients and the 4 egg yolks. Leave to rest for about 20 minutes, covered with a towel. Chop the vegetables. Place a large skillet over a medium heat with the butter and the oil, and sauté the vegetables for 3–4 minutes, until they start to color. Add the meat and fry for 5 minutes or so, until nicely browned. Add the wine and the Marsala. Cook until it has evaporated completely. Season with salt and pepper to taste.
Warm through the béchamel.
Cook the macaroni in lightly salted boiling water. Drain when *al dente* and dress with the béchamel and the ragù, and sprinkle with the grated Parmigiano, mixing together with great care. Roll out the pastry to a thickness of ⅛ in (2 mm) and line the bottom and the sides of a suitable pie mold, previously buttered and floured. Fill the mold with the macaroni, dress and garnish with the truffle if preferred. Cover with another round of pasta and seal the edges. Brush the surface with egg yolk mixed with a little water. Place in the oven at 400°F (200°C) and serve when the surface is golden brown.

Italian Region: Emilia-Romagna.

PENNE A CANDELA CON PESCE SPADA E POMODORINI
PENNE WITH SWORDFISH AND CHERRY TOMATOES

Difficulty 1

Ingredients for 4 people
Preparation time: 30' (preparation: 15' – cooking: 15')

14 oz (400 g) penne
7 oz (200 g) swordfish
7 oz (200 g) cherry tomatoes
2 cloves garlic
2 tsp chopped parsley
1 pinch chilli powder
¼ cup (50 ml) extra virgin olive oil
Salt

Method

Coarsely chop up the fish. Chop the tomatoes. Place a skillet onto a medium heat. Add the oil and the garlic, cook slowly until it starts to color. Then add the swordfish and stir for a couple of minutes, followed by the tomatoes, the parsley, and the chilli pepper. Cook for a further 2 minutes. Season with salt to taste.
Cook the pasta in a large pan of lightly salted boiling water and drain when *al dente*. Toss the pasta in the prepared sauce.

Italian Region: Calabria.

PENNE LISCE ALLE MELANZANE E PESCE SPADA
PENNE WITH EGGPLANT AND SWORDFISH

Difficulty 1

Ingredients for 4 people
Preparation time: 40' (preparation: 20' – cooking: 20')

14 oz (400 g) penne lisce
⅔ cup (150 ml) extra virgin olive oil
7 oz (200 g) eggplant (aubergine)
7 oz (200 g) swordfish
8 leaves basil
5 oz (150 g) cherry tomatoes
⅓ cup (80 ml) white wine
5 oz (150 g) salted ricotta
1 clove garlic
Salt
Pepper

Method

Wash the eggplants (aubergines) and cut into cubes. Place a large skillet with ½ cup (100 ml) of oil onto a high heat and when hot, fry the eggplant. As soon as they are golden, drain them using a slotted spoon and dry them on absorbent paper; keep warm. Chop the garlic. Cut up the swordfish into cubes. Heat the remaining oil in a large skillet over a medium heat, add the garlic, the fish, and brown for a few minutes. Wash the tomatoes, cut into half, and add to the pan with the fish. Stir well, add the wine and cook until completely evaporated. Add the basil, torn into pieces by hand, and season with salt and pepper. Cook the pasta in abundant boiling salted water. Drain when *al dente*. Toss the pasta with the prepared sauce, the fried eggplant, the salted ricotta and serve.

Chef's Tips

The cubes of eggplant must be fried in very hot oil so as to form a crust immediately, to stop them absorbing the oil.

In this recipe, one of the most prized fish in Sicilian gastronomy is combined with the most typical vegetable in the island's cuisine to create a dish with an intriguing and delicate flavor.

Italian Region: Sicily.

FOOD HISTORY

Although swordfish is often caught using modern fishing systems, in the Straight of Messina, the corridor between Sicily and the rest of Italy, swordfish is still caught with a harpoon. This method has been used for more than 2,000 years and is truly a sight to behold. Practiced with a technique that has hardly changed over the centuries, harpooning is a form of hunting that is, above all, one that is full of rituals and secrets.

Harpooning takes place off special motorboats—20-ft (6-m) long feluccas, equipped with powerful motors that allow the boats to reach very high speeds. They are characterized by a gangplank between 65 to 130 ft (20–40m) long, reaching out from the bow, and an enormous mast, some 100 ft (30 m) high. These are perfect hunting boats: Once the swordfish is spotted, it has no chance of escaping.

High on top of the tall mast, there is equipment used to guide the boat, including a seat for the helmsman, who must have great courage and particularly good vision. The helmsman must spend the entire day looking for swordfish and, once the target is in sight, he has to both warn the rest of the crew and guide the boat near to the fish. Once the helmsman gets the boat close enough, the "u lanzaturi" are put into action. Positioned at the very end of the plank, the fishermen launch the harpoons with great force in order to capture the swordfish.

PENNE RIGATE ALLA NORMA
NORMA'S PENNE RIGATE

Difficulty 2

Ingredients for 4 people
Preparation time: 45' (preparation: 30' – cooking: 15')

14 oz (400 g) penne rigate
9 oz (250 g) eggplants (aubergines)
3 oz (80 g) salted ricotta
7 oz (200 g) tomato pulp
2 oz (50 g) onion

2 tbs (30 ml) extra virgin olive oil
6 leaves basil
1 clove garlic
Salt
Pepper

Method

Cut the eggplant (aubergines) into cubes and sprinkle lightly with salt.
Leave to rest for 20 minutes or so, until the juices have had a chance to
drain out. Toss in flour and fry in plenty of olive oil. Chop the onion and
garlic. Place a large skillet over a medium heat. Add the oil and, when hot,
sauté the onion and garlic until they start to color.

Add the eggplant, the tomato pulp, salt, and pepper, and cook for 15
minutes or so.
Cook the pasta in lightly salted boiling water. Drain when *al dente* and
dress with the prepared sauce.
Finish the dish with the basil and the grated salted ricotta. Serve very hot.

Chef's Tips

Before sautéing vegetables such as eggplant or zucchini, it is best to slice
them, place them in a colander, and sprinkle them with salt.
This removes the excess liquid contained in the vegetables and they will
be sweeter and crisper after cooking.

Italian Region: Sicily.

FOOD HISTORY

*A tasty and colorful recipe originally from Catania, Pasta alla Norma is a triumph of
Mediterranean flavors and was so called in honor of Vincenzo Bellini's opera "Norma."
It is said that Nino Martoglio, a Sicilian writer and poet, was so impressed when he
first tasted this dish that he compared it to "Norma," Bellini's masterpiece.
And the name has persisted ever since.*

PENNE RIGATE IN SALSA EOLIANA
PENNE RIGATE WITH AEOLIAN-STYLE SAUCE

Difficulty 1

Ingredients for 4 people
Preparation time: 25' (preparation: 10' – cooking: 15')

14 oz (400 g) penne rigate
4 oz (100 g) capers in brine
2 oz (50 g) pitted green olives
2 oz (50 g) pitted black olives
6 San Marzano tomatoes
1 clove garlic
3 leaves basil
2 tbs (40 ml) extra virgin olive oil
1 pinch chilli powder
1 tsp chopped oregano
Salt

Method

Rinse the capers and chop them finely together with the pitted olives.
In a skillet, heat half the oil and sauté the garlic over a low heat. Just as the garlic begins to color, remove and add the finely chopped capers and olives. Sauté gently for 2 minutes. Skin and deseed the tomatoes, then chop roughly. Add to the skillet and continue cooking for around 10 minutes.
Toward the end of cooking, add to the sauce the oregano, the basil leaves torn up by hand, and a pinch of chilli. Stir well and season with salt to taste. Cook the penne in lightly salted boiling water and drain when *al dente*. Toss with the prepared sauce and the remaining oil and serve.

This flavorful sauce, which is easy and quick to prepare, takes its name from the archipelago to the north of the Gulf of Patti. There is another version, a "white" one without the tomatoes, based solely on capers, garlic, and tuna in oil that has been drained.

Italian Region: Sicily.

PENNETTE ALLE CIPOLLE
PENNETTE WITH ONIONS

Difficulty 1

Ingredients for 4 people
Preparation time: 15' (preparation: 5' – cooking: 10')

14 oz (400 g) pennette
2 medium onions
1½ oz (40 g) grated Parmigiano
8 tsp milk
4 tsp (20 ml) extra virgin olive oil
Salt
Pepper

Method

Peel the onions, wash, and slice finely. Place them in a medium-sized pan on the stove and add a little salt. Cover and cook on a very low heat for at least 10 minutes.

Remove the lid and add two spoonfuls of milk. Cook the pasta in salted boiling water and drain when *al dente*. Dress at once with the onions once they have softened.

Combine well. Add the grated Parmigiano and the olive oil. Season generously with pepper and serve immediately.

PERCIATELLI LAZIALI CACIO E BROCCOLI
PERCIATELLI LAZIALI WITH CHEESE AND BROCCOLI

Difficulty 1

Ingredients for 4 people
Preparation time: 30' (preparation: 10' – cooking: 20')

1 lb 2 oz (500 g) perciatelli laziali
1 lb 2 oz (500 g) broccoli
7 oz (200 g) Provola
2 tbs (40 ml) extra virgin olive oil
¼ oz (10 g) butter
Salt

Method

Slice the Provola or Cacio and reserve.
Trim the broccoli, wash, and break apart into florets. Heat the oil in a skillet over a low heat. Add the broccoli and cook for 10 minutes, adding a little water from time to time to prevent it sticking to the pan. Season with salt and keep warm. Meanwhile, cook the pasta in lightly salted boiling water and drain when *al dente*. Transfer to a buttered baking dish and dress with the broccoli and the slices of Provola cheese. Place in the oven at 360°F (180°C) for about 10 minutes, or until the top becomes golden. Remove from the oven and serve.

Chef's Tips

There are innumerable variations of pasta "ncaciata" that traditionally uses cacio cheese. Some, apart from using broccoli and cheese, add a sausage meat sauce or one made from some other pork meat. Instead of broccoli, eggplant can be used or, even peas and boiled egg cut into slices.

REGINETTE AL PROSCIUTTO E PORRI
REGINETTE WITH HAM AND LEEKS

Difficulty 1

Ingredients for 4 people
Preparation time: 20' (preparation: 10' – cooking: 10')

14 oz (400 g) reginette
9 oz (250 g) two slices cooked ham
2 leeks
2 cups (500 ml) white wine
4 oz (100 g) béchamel
2 oz (50 g) grated Parmigiano
2 tbs (40 ml) extra virgin olive oil
Salt
Pepper

Method

Clean the leeks, removing the green part. Halve lengthwise. Cut each half into ⅛ in (3 mm) thick strips. Cut the ham into small cubes of ½ in (10 mm). Heat the oil in a large skillet over a medium heat, add the leek, and cook for a couple of minutes until it browns. Add the diced ham, and fry gently for a further 2 minutes until it starts to color, stirring all the time. Pour over the wine and allow it to evaporate completely. Simmer for another 5 minutes and season with salt and pepper.
Cook the pasta in a pan of lightly salted boiling water. Drain when *al dente*. Dress with the prepared sauce and the béchamel sauce, and sprinkle with the Parmigiano. Serve immediately.

RIGATONI AI QUATTRO FORMAGGI
RIGATONI WITH FOUR CHEESES

Difficulty 1

Ingredients for 4 people
Preparation time: 25' (preparation: 15' – cooking: 10')

14 oz (400 g) rigatoni
3 oz (80 g) Gorgonzola
3 oz (80 g) Edam
3 oz (80 g) Gruyère
4 oz (100 g) Parmigiano
4 oz (100 g) butter
Salt
Pepper

Method

Cut the Gorgonzola, Edam, Gruyère, and half the Parmigiano into small pieces. Grate the rest of the Parmigiano.

Then, place the butter in in a bain marie over half a liter of very hot water, to melt and keep warm.
Cook the pasta in a large pan of lightly salted boiling water and drain when *al dente*. Dress with all the small pieces of cheese, half the grated Parmigiano, and half of the melted butter.

Arrange the dressed rigatoni on a serving dish, adding the other half of the grated Parmigiano and the remaining butter. Serve immediately so that the four cheeses do not have time to melt completely.

RIGATONI ALLA RICCA
RICH RIGATONI

Difficulty 1

Ingredients for 4 people
Preparation time: 35' (preparation: 20' – cooking: 15')

14 oz (400 g) rigatoni
2½ oz (60 g) prosciutto fat
1 small onion
2½ oz (60 g) chicken livers
2½ oz (60 g) porcini mushrooms
1½ oz (40 g) prosciutto
10 oz (300 g) tomato pulp

½ cup (100 ml) red wine
1½ oz (40 g) butter
4 oz (100 g) grated Parmigiano
4 leaves basil
Salt
Pepper

Method

Finely chop the onion and the prosciutto fat, cube the mushrooms and the chicken livers, and cut the prosciutto into small strips. Place a large skillet over a moderate heat with the prosciutto fat and soften the onion in it, without allowing it to color. Add the mushrooms and the livers and cook for a couple of minutes until they brown. Add the prosciutto and, immediately after, the tomato pulp.

Cook for about 10–12 minutes. Season with salt and pepper. In the meantime, place a small pan over a medium heat. Pour in the wine and cook until almost completely reduced. Add this to the tomato pulp.
Cook the rigatoni in lightly salted boiling water.
Drain when *al dente* and dress with the prepared sauce, the butter and the Parmigiano, and serve.

RIGATONI CON SALSICCE E UOVA
RIGATONI WITH SAUSAGE AND EGGS

Difficulty 1

Ingredients for 4 people
Preparation time: 25' (preparation: 10' – cooking: 15')

14 oz (400 g) rigatoni
4 oz (100 g) butter
2 tsp (10 ml) extra virgin olive oil
4 pork sausages
¼ cup (50 ml) meat stock
2 eggs
2½ oz (60 g) Parmigiano
Salt

Method

Place a skillet over a moderate heat with half the butter and the oil.
Remove the skin from the sausages, then add the meat to the skillet,
breaking it up with a wooden spoon. Cook gently and from time to time
pour in a few tablespoons of stock, so that the sauce does not become too
dry. In the meantime, beat the eggs in a mixing bowl with a pinch of salt
and half the Parmigiano. Cook the rigatoni in lightly salted boiling water.
Drain and dress with the sausage ragù, the butter, and the remaining
Parmigiano. Remove the pan from the heat, add the beaten eggs, and stir
until the eggs become creamy. Serve.

RIGATONI ROMANI CACIO E PEPE
RIGATONI ROMAN STYLE WITH CHEESE AND PEPPER

Difficulty 1

Ingredients for 4 people
Preparation time: 15' (preparation: 5' – cooking: 10')

14 oz (400 g) rigatoni
2 tbs (40 ml) extra virgin olive oil
4 oz (100 g) grated Pecorino
3 tsp pepper ground in a mortar
Salt

Method

Cook the pasta in lightly salted boiling water and drain when *al dente*. Coat the pasta with the extra virgin olive oil, the grated Pecorino, the pepper, and a ladle of the reserved pasta cooking water. Serve.

RUOTE CON CIPOLLA DI TROPEA
RUOTE WITH TROPEA ONIONS

Difficulty 1

Ingredients for 4 people
Preparation time: 20' (preparation: 10' – cooking: 10')

14 oz (400 g) ruote
6 tropea onions
1 red bell pepper
6 leaves basil
1 cup (200 ml) tomato sauce
2½ oz (60 g) grated Parmigiano
¼ cup (50 ml) extra virgin olive oil
Salt
Pepper

Method

Peel the onion and cut into thin slices. Heat the oil in a skillet over a
medium heat. Add the onions and cook to soften for 2–3 minutes. Halve
the bell pepper, remove the seeds, and cut into chunks. Add to the skillet.
Tear the basil leaves into pieces by hand, then add and cook for a couple
more minutes. Add the tomato sauce, adjust the salt, and cook for a
further 5 minutes. Cook the pasta in lightly salted boiling water and drain
when *al dente*. Toss with the prepared sauce. Add the Parmigiano and
freshly ground black pepper. Serve.

Italian Region: Calabria.

SCHIAFFONI AL GUANCIALE
SCHIAFFONI WITH BACON SAUCE

Difficulty 1

Ingredients for 4 people
Preparation time: 20' (preparation: 10' – cooking: 10')

14 oz (400 g) schiaffoni
5 oz (150 g) bacon
1 clove garlic
4 tsp (20 ml) extra virgin olive
2 tsp chopped parsley
2 oz (50 g) grated Pecorino
½ cup (100 ml) dry white wine
Paprika (optional)
Salt
Pepper

Method

Tenderize two-thirds of the bacon by beating it. Place it in a skillet on a medium heat with the clove of garlic. When the bacon becomes golden brown, add the wine and allow the liquid to evaporate completely. Cut the rest of the bacon into small pieces and add to the pan. Cook the pasta in lightly salted boiling water and drain when *al dente*. Coat with the prepared sauce, the chopped parsley, the grated Pecorino, some freshly ground pepper, and the paprika. Toss and serve.

Italian Region: Basilicata.

SEDANI MARI E MONTI
SEDANI WITH SHELLFISH AND MUSHROOMS

Difficulty 1

Ingredients for 4 people
Preparation time: 22' (preparation: 10' – cooking: 12')

14 oz (400 g) sedani
1 lb 2 oz (500 g) mussels
1 lb 2 oz (500g) clams
4 oz (100 g) dried porcini mushrooms
2 tsp chopped parsley
⅓ cup (80 ml) extra virgin olive oil
Salt
Pepper

Method

Scrape the mussels with a knife, rinse, and place in a pan with a few spoonfuls of oil. Heat and when they have all opened, remove them from their shells and place them in a bowl together with a ladle of the filtered cooking water. Rinse the clams carefully and heat them to open in a pan in the same way. Remove from their shells, strain the cooking water, and combine with the mussels.

Soak the dried mushrooms in warm water.
Heat a little oil in a skillet over a medium heat, add the mushrooms, and cook until they begin to color. Add a little of the cooking water from the mussels and the clams, and continue cooking for a few minutes. Add the remaining cooking stock, the mussels, and the clams; turn off the heat. Cook the pasta in lightly salted boiling water and drain when *al dente*. Dress with the prepared sauce and the chopped parsley.

SEDANINI VEGETARIANI
VEGETARIAN SEDANINI

Difficulty 1

Ingredients for 4 people
Preparation time: 45' (preparation: 25' – cooking: 20')

14 oz (400 g) sedanini
1 lb 2 oz (500 g) tomatoes
1 carrot
1 stick celery
1 onion
1 leek
1 clove garlic
1 dried chilli
¼ cup (60 ml) extra virgin olive oil
Salt

Method

Skin, seed and cut the tomatoes into small cubes.
Wash the rest of the vegetables. Cut half of them into matchstick-sized pieces and reserve. Coarsely chop the remainder of the vegetables.
Heat the oil in a large skillet over a low heat. Add the roughly chopped vegetables and the whole garlic, and fry until softened.
When the vegetables are soft, add the tomatoes and season with the crumbled chilli. Continue cooking for 10 minutes on a low heat. Adjust the seasoning and blend everything in a food processor. Keep the sauce warm.
Cook the sedanini in lightly salted boiling water and drain when *al dente*.
Dress with the vegetable sauce, the raw vegetables, and the remaining oil.
Serve immediately.

SPACCATELLE AL NERO DI SEPPIA
SPACCATELLE WITH CUTTLEFISH INK

Difficulty 1

Ingredients for 4 people
Preparation time: 30' (preparation: 10' – cooking: 20')

14 oz (400 g) spaccatelle
1 4oz (400 g) cuttlefish
7 oz (200 g) peeled tomatoes
2 tbs (40 ml) extra virgin olive oil
2 cloves garlic
Salt
Black pepper

Method

Wash and clean the cuttlefish. Remove the ink sacs from the cuttlefish without breaking them, then dice the cuttlefish. Place a large skillet onto a medium heat, add the oil, and lightly brown the cloves of garlic, left whole. Add the cuttlefish and allow to brown for a few minutes. Season with salt and pepper. Add the contents of the broken up ink sacs and the tomatoes. Continue cooking for a further 10 minutes. Adjust the seasoning.

Cook the pasta in lightly salted boiling water and drain when *al dente*. Dress with the prepared sauce.

SPACCATELLE CON LE SARDE
SPACCATELLE WITH SARDINES

Difficulty 2

Ingredients for 4 people
Preparation time: 1 h (preparation: 30' – cooking: 30')

14 oz (400 g) spaccatelle
1 bunch wild fennel
1 onion
½ cup (100 ml) extra virgin olive oil
4 desalted anchovies
14 oz (400 g) fresh sardines
1 oz (25 g) raisins
1 oz (25 g) pine nuts
¾ oz (20 g) toasted and ground almonds
1 pinch saffron
2½ oz (60 g) breadcrumbs
Oil for frying
Salt
Pepper

Method

Clean and cook the wild fennel in lightly salted water for 15 minutes from the time it comes to the boil. Drain and reserve the cooking water. Squeeze out any excess water from the fennel and cut into small chunks of ½-1 in (10-20 mm). Chop the onion. Bone the anchovies. Clean and bone the sardines, reserving 4 left open like a book. Toast the breadcrumbs in a small dry skillet. Place a large skillet over a medium heat with the oil and when hot, add the onion and cook until it starts to color. Combine with the anchovies, breaking them up with a fork. Add the fresh sardines, the raisins, the pine nuts, the ground toasted almonds, and cook for around 10 minutes. Season with salt and pepper to taste. Now add the fennel and a pinch of saffron, and stir carefully. Lower the heat and continue cooking for another 10 minutes. Fry the 4 fresh sardines separately, without flour. Finally, cook the pasta in the fennel cooking water; drain when *al dente*. Now dress the pasta with the sauce of sardines and fennel, and arrange it in a greased ovenproof dish. Sprinkle the surface with the breadcrumbs and cover with the 4 fried sardines. Place in a very hot oven at 425°F (220°C) for 8–10 minutes.

SPAGHETTI AGLIO, OLIO E PEPERONCINO
SPAGHETTI WITH GARLIC, OIL AND CHILI

Difficulty 1

Ingredients for 4 people
Preparation time: 22' (preparation: 10' – cooking: 12')

14 oz (400 g) spaghetti
4 oz (100 g) extra virgin olive oil
3 cloves garlic
Hot chilli pepper
2 tsp chopped parsley
Salt

Method

Heat the oil in a skillet over a medium heat. Add the garlic and the chilli pepper. Just as the garlic cloves begin to color, remove from the pan and add the chopped parsley.

Cook the pasta in lightly salted boiling water. Drain when *al dente* and dress with the prepared sauce.

Italian Region: Abruzzo.

SPAGHETTI AL CARTOCCIO
SPAGHETTI BAKED IN FOIL

Difficulty 1

Ingredients for 4 people
Preparation time: 40' (preparation: 20' – cooking: 20')

14 oz (400 g) spaghetti
¼ cup (50 ml) extra virgin olive oil
2 cloves garlic
4 tsp chopped parsley
8 scampi
1 lb 2oz (500 g) clams
4 calamari
¼ cup (50 ml) white wine
7 oz (200 g) tomatoes
1 dried chilli
Salt

Method

Put a casserole onto a medium heat with half the oil and the clams. Cover and wait until they open. Shell the clams and keep warm. Filter the liquid through a very fine cloth/gauze and reserve. Remove the shells of the scampi. Clean, wash, and slice the calamari.
Heat the remaining oil in a large skillet over a medium heat. Add the garlic and, as soon as it begins to color, add all the shellfish. Brown for 2 minutes. Add the wine and cook until it has completely evaporated. Skin, seed, and shop the tomatoes into little cubes. Add to the pan with the crumbled dried chilli and the clam water. Cook for about 10 minutes. Cook the pasta in lightly salted boiling water and drain a couple of minutes before done. Dress with the prepared sauce and sprinkle over the chopped parsley.
Take a sheet of aluminum foil about 32 in (80 cm) long and fold over. Arrange the spaghetti on the foil sheet and cover with another sheet of foil the same size. Seal the edges by folding them over 3 or 4 times. Bake in the oven at 360°F (180°C) for about 5 minutes.
If wished, ovenproof paper can be used instead of aluminum foil for the top.

Italian Region: Abruzzo.

SPAGHETTI ALLA CARBONARA
SPAGHETTI WITH CARBONARA SAUCE

Difficulty 1

Ingredients for 4 people
Preparation time: 15' (preparation: 10' – cooking: 5')

14 oz (400 g) spaghetti
5 oz (150 g) bacon or pancetta
4 egg yolks
4 oz (100 g) Pecorino

4 tsp (20 ml) extra virgin olive oil
Salt
Pepper

Method

Beat the egg yolks with a pinch of salt and a little Pecorino in a bowl. Cut the bacon into small strips. Place a large skillet onto a medium heat and slowly sauté the bacon. Cook the spaghetti in a pot of lightly salted boiling water and drain when *al dente*. Turn the pasta into the skillet with the bacon, toss, and turn off the heat. Add the beaten egg yolks and a little of the cooking water. Stir for 30 seconds or so. Add the remaining Pecorino, stir again, and serve immediately.

Italian Region: Lazio.

FOOD HISTORY

Pasta alla carbonara is one of the most famous Italian dishes worldwide. And as is often the case with famous recipes, there are many legends surrounding the origins of this dish. Despite being a fairly recent creation, there are a lot of theories, often contradictory, about how this dish came into existence.

There are two main theories: The most famous suggests that pasta alla carbonara was invented during World War II when someone tried to make a pasta dish using the ingredients rationed to the American soldiers—namely eggs and bacon—to toss with the pasta, adding pepper and cheese at the end for more flavor.

The second theory, instead, suggests that carbonara is the evolution of an ancient Roman dish called "cacio e ova" (or cheese and egg) that was served to the coal miners or carbonari.

Even if cheese and egg had been used with pasta for a long time, this recipe became the carbonara as we know it today during World War II when the American soldiers asked the tavern cooks to add guanciale (or cured pork jowl) which they mistook for bacon, something Americans commonly pair with eggs.

According to the most accredited theories, the name "carbonara" comes from the presence of ground black pepper. In the traditional recipe, it is said that so much pepper was used that it looked like powdered carbon.

Eggs, bacon, and pepper give this dish its intense, but delicate taste. Spaghetti alla carbonara is one of the most famous Italian recipes worldwide.

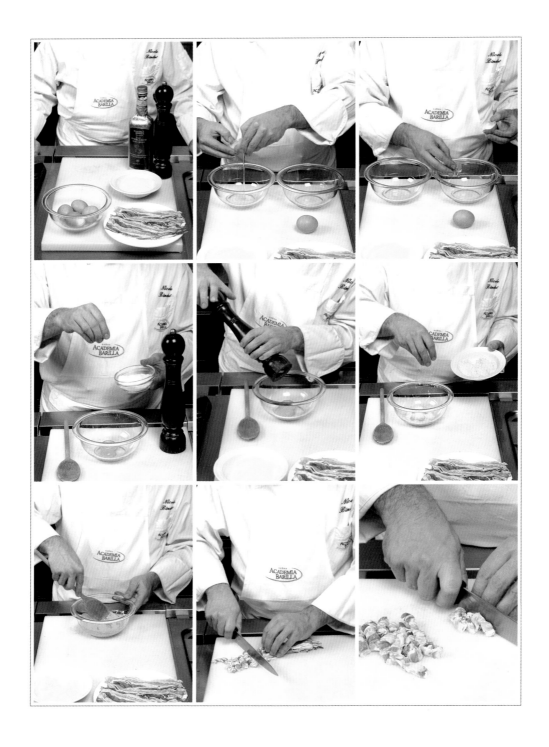

SEMOLINA PASTA • 161

SPAGHETTI ALLA GENNARO

SPAGHETTI GENNARO

Difficulty 1

Ingredients for 4 people
Preparation time: 15' (preparation: 7' – cooking: 8)

14 oz (400 g) spaghetti
¼ cup (50 ml) extra virgin olive oil
3 slices stale bread
4 desalted anchovies

6 leaves basil
3 cloves garlic
2 tsp chopped oregano
Salt

Method

Rub the bread slices with 1 clove of garlic, then crumble them onto a plate. Heat half the oil in a skillet over a medium heat, add the other two whole garlic cloves, and the bread. Gently sauté the bread, being careful that the garlic does not become too brown.
Heat the remaining oil in another skillet over a medium heat. Chop the anchovies and add them with the oregano. Cook for two minutes. Cook the pasta in lightly salted boiling water and drain when *al dente*. Dress with the prepared sauce, the crispy bread, the basil leaves torn up by hand, and stir quickly. Serve at once.

This recipe comes from a cookbook that Liliana De Curtis dedicated to her father. It is a simple "peasant" dish that captures the Neapolitan spirit that Toto portrayed on the big screen and the stage alike.

Italian Region: Campania.

SPAGHETTI ALLA GHIOTTA
GLUTTON'S SPAGHETTI

Difficulty 2

Ingredients for 4 people
Preparation time: 40' (preparation: 20' – cooking: 20')

14 oz (400 g) spaghetti
7 oz (200 g) meat sauce
1 onion
2 oz (50 g) chicken
2 oz (50 g) prosciutto
2 tomatoes
4 oz (100 g) eggplant

½ cup (100 ml) oil for frying
4 oz (100 g) mozzarella
1½ oz (40 g) butter
1 tbs brandy
2½ oz (60 g) grated Parmigiano
Salt
Pepper

Method

Chop the onion. Chop chicken and prosciutto into cubes. Heat half the butter in a skillet over a medium heat. Add the onion. Just as it begins to color, add the chicken and the prosciutto. Cook for 2 minutes, pour in the brandy, and simmer until completely evaporated. Finely slice the tomatoes and add to the skillet. Continue cooking for about 8 minutes. Season with salt and pepper, and keep warm with the ragù (keeping the dressings separate). Wash and cut the eggplant into slices. Heat the oil in a skillet over a high heat and fry the eggplant; remove and keep warm. Cook the pasta in lightly salted boiling water and drain when *al dente*. Arrange in an ovenproof dish and dot little pats of butter. Sprinkle with half the Parmigiano. Cut the mozzarella into slices and add, together with half of the two sauces, still warm. Stir carefully. Serve, with the remainder of the sauces and the Parmigiano served separately.

SPAGHETTI ALLA "GRICIA"
SPAGHETTI WITH BACON

Difficulty 1

Ingredients for 4 people
Preparation time: 20' (preparation: 10' – cooking: 10')

14 oz (400 g) spaghetti
¼ cup (50 ml) olive oil
10 oz (300 g) bacon or pancetta
Fresh chilli pepper
5 oz (140 g) grated Pecorino
Salt

Method

Heat the oil in a large skillet over a medium heat. Cut the bacon into small pieces and add. Season with chilli to taste and sauté slowly for 3 minutes. Cook the pasta in lightly salted boiling water and drain when *al dente*. Dress with the prepared sauce, sprinkle with the grated Pecorino, and serve.

Italian Region: Lazio.

SPAGHETTI ALLA NURSINA
SPAGHETTI WITH TRUFFLE

Difficulty 1

Ingredients for 4 people
Preparation time: 20' (preparation: 10' – cooking: 10')

14 oz (400 g) spaghetti
½ cup (100 ml) extra virgin olive oil
3 oz (80 g) black truffle
1 clove garlic
1 salted anchovy
10 leaves basil
Salt

Method

Clean the truffle by brushing it carefully. Slice it using the special tool, and cut up half of the slivers obtained with a knife.

Place a pan onto a low heat with half of the oil, adding the cut pieces of truffle and 4 leaves of basil, torn up by hand. Put another medium-sized skillet onto a low heat with the remaining oil, adding the garlic in its skin (unpeeled). Combine with the desalted, chopped anchovy, broken up in the oil. Remove the garlic. Cook the pasta in lightly salted boiling water and drain when *al dente*. Dress the pasta with the anchovy sauce and the truffle crushed in its oil, the rest of the basil, and the reserved truffle slivers. Serve at once.

Italian Region: Umbria.

SPAGHETTI ALLA PUTTANESCA
SPAGHETTI WITH PUTTANESCA SAUCE

Difficulty 1

Ingredients for 4 people
Preparation time: 30' (preparation: 20' – cooking: 10')

14 oz (400 g) spaghetti
1¼ oz (30 g) butter
2 tbs (30 ml) extra virgin olive oil
4 desalted anchovies, pounded in a mortar with a pestle
4 thinly sliced cloves garlic
5 oz (150 g) pitted black olives
2 tsp rinsed and roughly chopped salted capers
1 tomato
2 tsp chopped parsley
Salt

Method

Place a large saucepan onto a moderate heat and melt the butter and olive oil. Add the thinly sliced garlic and pounded anchovies.

Chop the olives; rinse and roughly chop the capers; skin, deseed, and slice the tomato. When the garlic begins to turn golden, add the olives, capers, and the tomato. Cook over a high heat for 2 minutes. Adjust the salt.

Cook the pasta in lightly salted boiling water and drain when *al dente*. Dress with the prepared sauce, add the chopped parsley, toss, and serve.

Italian Region: Lazio.

SPAGHETTI CON AGLIO E POMODORO
SPAGHETTI WITH GARLIC AND TOMATO

Difficulty 1

Ingredients for 4 people
Preparation time: 20' (preparation: 10' – cooking: 10')

14 oz (400 g) spaghetti
1¼ lb (600 g) tomatoes
2 tbs (40 ml) extra virgin olive oil
1 clove garlic
Salt

Method

Heat the oil in a skillet over a medium heat and sauté the garlic, removing
it just as it starts to color. Skin, seed, and cut the tomatoes into little cubes.
Add to the pan. Simmer for 10 minutes or so and season to taste.
Cook the pasta in lightly salted boiling water and drain when *al dente*.
Dress with the prepared sauce and serve.

SPAGHETTI CON AGLIO, OLIO E ALICI
SPAGHETTI WITH GARLIC, OIL, AND ANCHOVIES

Difficulty 1

Ingredients for 4 people
Preparation time: 20' (preparation: 10' – cooking: 10')

14 oz (400 g) spaghetti
2 tbs (40 ml) extra virgin olive oil
2 cloves garlic
6 fresh anchovies
2 tsp hopped parsley
Salt
Pepper

Method

Heat the oil in a skillet over a medium heat and add the cloves of garlic. Remove the garlic as soon as it starts to color. Add to the pan the washed anchovies, boned and chopped into pieces. Sauté for 2 minutes. Remove the skillet from the stove and crush the anchovies with the prongs of a fork. Season with pepper and add the chopped parsley. Cook the pasta in lightly salted boiling water and drain when *al dente*. Dress with the prepared sauce and serve.

SPAGHETTI CON LE VONGOLE
SPAGHETTI WITH CLAMS

Difficulty 1

Ingredients for 4 people
Preparation time: 35' (preparation: 20' – cooking: 15')

14 oz (400 g) spaghetti
1¾ lb (800 g) clams
14 oz (400 g) tomatoes
1 clove garlic
¼ cup (50 ml) extra virgin olive oil
1 spoonful chopped parsley
Salt
Pepper

Method

Carefully wash the clams. Heat half the oil in a large skillet over a medium heat, add the clams, and cover. Cook for about 5 minutes and the clams will open with the heat. When they are open, remove from the heat, keep warm and remove from their shells, reserving the cooking liquid. Heat the remaining oil in another skillet over a medium heat, crush the clove of garlic, and add. Skin, deseed, and cut the tomatoes into pieces. When the garlic is golden, remove it, and add the tomatoes. Add the clam liquid, filtered through a fine gauze/cloth, and cook for around 10 minutes. Season with salt. Cook the pasta in lightly salted boiling water and drain when *al dente*. Dress with the prepared sauce, sprinkle over the parsley and a generous amount of pepper. Serve at once.

There is a variation: Spaghetti with clams can also be prepared "in bianco" with a white sauce. In this recipe, cook to open the clams, filter the water, and reserve. In a skillet, sauté lightly two cloves of garlic in half a glass of oil. Remove the garlic, add the clams and their water. Bring to the boil. Dress the spaghetti with the sauce, garnish with the chopped parsley, and season with pepper.

Italian Region: Campania.

SPAGHETTI TAGLIATI E LENTICCHIE
SPAGHETTI PIECES WITH LENTILS

Difficulty 2

Ingredients for 4 people
Preparation time: 1 h (preparation: 30' – cooking: 30')

9 oz (250 g) spaghetti
10 oz (300 g) lentils
4 oz (100 g) celery
2 cloves garlic
4 oz (100 g) onion
10 oz (300 g) peeled tomatoes
¼ cup (50 ml) extra virgin olive oil
Salt
Pepper

Method

Clean and rinse the lentils. Chop the celery and the onion. Place a pan, preferably a crock-pot, over a medium heat. Add the oil and when hot, the celery, the onion, and the garlic. Cook for 5 minutes and then add the peeled tomatoes.

When the sauce has reduced considerably, add the lentils and the water. Continue cooking the lentils, leaving enough water in which to cook the pasta. Break the spaghetti into pieces of about ½ in (2 cm) each and cook until done. Finish the dish with the remaining oil. Serve hot with plenty of black pepper.

Italian Region: Apulia.

TOFARELLE ALLE TRIGLIE

TOFARELLE WITH RED MULLET

Difficulty 1

Ingredients for 4 people
Preparation time: 40' (preparation: 20 – cooking: 20')

14 oz (400 g) tofarelle
8 red mullet
3 sardines
1 clove garlic
9 oz (250 g) tomato passata
1 tbs chopped parsley
5 tbs extra virgin olive oil
1 sprig thyme
1 pinch chilli powder
Salt

Method

Clean and carefully wash the red mullet, removing the guts and the scales.
Remove the head and the bones from the sardines, and cut into pieces.
Heat the oil in a skillet over a medium heat, add the crushed garlic, the
sardine pieces, the tomato passata, the stripped thyme leaves, the salt,
and the chilli. Cook for 10 minutes. Add the mullet and cook for another 10
minutes. Remove the mullet. Sprinkle the chopped parsley into the sauce.
Cook the pasta in lightly salted boiling water and drain when *al dente*.
Dress with the prepared sauce.

Italian Region: Marche.

TORTIGLIONI AL GORGONZOLA
TORTIGLIONI WITH GORGONZOLA

Difficulty 1

Ingredients for 4 people
Preparation time: 22' (preparation: 10' – cooking: 12')

14 oz (400 g) tortiglioni
10 oz (280 g) Gorgonzola
1½ oz (40 g) cream
3 oz (80 g) grated Parmigiano
Salt

Method

Cut the Gorgonzola into little cubes and place in a ceramic or stainless steel bowl. Warm a pan with water over a low heat, and place the bowl with the Gorgonzola over it so it comes into contact with the water.

Melt the cheese in this bain marie, stirring with a whisk. Add the cream and the Parmigiano. Cook the pasta in lightly salted boiling water and drain when *al dente*. Dress with the prepared sauce.

TORTIGLIONI CON BROCCOLI E SALSICCIA
TORTIGLIONI WITH BROCCOLI AND SAUSAGE

Difficulty 1

Ingredients for 4 people
Preparation time: 25' (preparation: 10' – cooking: 15')

14 oz (400 g) tortiglioni
7 oz (200 g) broccoli
1 clove garlic
1 pinch sweet chilli pepper
5 oz (150 g) pork sausage

1 salted anchovy (optional)
¼ cup (50 ml) extra virgin olive oil
1½ oz (40 g) grated Parmigiano
Salt
Pepper

Method

Heat the oil in a skillet over medium heat, add the garlic and sauté until lightly golden in color. Bone and rinse the anchovy in water, then add. After a few seconds, add the sausage, and continue cooking until browned. Season with salt, pepper, and chilli powder.

Wash and trim the broccoli, reserving only the florets. Cook the pasta and the broccoli in a large pan of lightly salted boiling water. Drain when *al dente* and toss with the prepared sausage. Sprinkle with the Parmigiano and serve.

Italian Region: Piedmont.

TRENETTE AL PESTO
TRENETTE WITH PESTO

Difficulty 1

Ingredients for 4 people
Preparation time: 20' (preparation: 10' – cooking: 10')

14 oz (400 g) trenette
1¼ oz (30 g) basil
½ oz (15 g) pine nuts
1 clove garlic
1 cup (200 ml) extra virgin olive oil
2½ oz (60 g) grated Parmigiano
1½ oz (40 g) grated Pecorino
Salt
Pepper

Method

To prepare the pesto alla genovese chop the garlic and the basil; add a pinch of salt to conserve the green color of the leaves. When the garlic and the basil have been finely chopped, place them in a mortar with the pine nuts. Pound the ingredients, perhaps adding a drizzle of oil to obtain a "pesto."
Transfer the pesto into a bowl and combine with all the other ingredients.

Cook the pasta in lightly salted boiling water and drain when *al dente*. Dress with the pesto and, if it seems too thick, dilute it with a glass of the pasta cooking water and serve.

TROCCOLI LUCANI ALLA JONICA
TROCCOLI WITH CHILIES AND TOMATO SAUCE

Difficulty 2

Ingredients for 4 people
Preparation time: 33' (preparation: 20' – cooking: 13')

14 oz (400 g) troccoli lucani
10 oz (300 g) fresh tomatoes
2 mild or hot chillies
2 cloves garlic
5 oz (140 g) bacon

8 leaves basil
2 oz (50 g) grated Pecorino
1¼ oz (30 g) extra virgin olive oil
Salt

Method

Wash the chillies and cut into pieces. Cook in boiling water for 2 minutes. Chop the tomatoes and parboil in water for 40 seconds. Cool in cold water, skin, cut into quarters, and remove the seeds. Dice the bacon.

Puree the chillies and tomatoes through a vegetable mill. Heat the oil in a skillet over a medium heat, add the garlic and the bacon, and fry gently.

Add the tomato and pepper sauce, and season with the basil. Cook the pasta in lightly salted boiling water and drain when *al dente*. Dress with the prepared sauce. Serve sprinkled with the grated Pecorino.

Italian Region: Calabria.

TROFIE ALLE NOCI
TROFIE WITH WALNUTS

Difficulty 1

Ingredients for 4 people
Preparation time: 15' (preparation: 5' – cooking: 10')

14 oz (400 g) trofie
5 oz (150 g) cream
2 oz (60 g) walnuts
1½ oz (40 g) butter
Ground nutmeg
Salt
Pepper

Method

Mill the walnut kernels with nutmeg, cream, and butter; season with salt and pepper. Cook the pasta in lightly salted boiling water and drain when *al dente*. Dress with the prepared sauce. If it seems too dry, add a few spoonfuls of the pasta cooking water.

This pasta is best served with a light sprinkling of breadcrumbs flavored with a little butter.

VERMICELLI AL PESTO ROSSO
VERMICELLI WITH RED PESTO

Difficulty 1

Ingredients for 4 people
Preparation time: 20' (preparation: 10' – cooking: 10')

14 oz (400 g) vermicelli
5 oz (150 g) sun-dried tomatoes in oil
1½ oz (45 g) pine nuts
1 clove garlic
2 tbs (30 ml) extra virgin olive oil
1½ oz (40 g) grated Parmigiano
Salt
Pepper

Method

Place the tomatoes, drained of their oil, with the clove of garlic and the pine nuts in an aluminum pan over medium heat. Cook, turning often.

When the pine nuts begin to change color, turn off the heat and transfer everything to a blender. Add the grated Parmigiano and blend until reduced to a homogeneous cream.

Add a generous twist of pepper and slowly incorporate the oil—the sauce should end up quite thick but with a fluid consistency. Cook the pasta in lightly salted boiling water and drain when *al dente*. Dress with the prepared sauce and serve.

VERMICELLI ALLA BERSAGLIERA
BERSAGLIERE-STYLE VERMICELLI

Difficulty 1

Ingredients for 4 people
Preparation time: 30' (preparation: 15' – cooking: 15')

14 oz (400 g) vermicelli
7 oz (200 g) salami
4 oz (100 g) provolone
14 oz (400 g) tomatoes
1 onion

4 tsp (20 ml) white wine
2 tbs (40 ml) extra virgin olive oil
1½ oz (40 g) grated Parmigiano
Salt

Method

Chop the onion; cut the salami into thin strips. Heat the oil in a skillet over a medium heat. Add the onion and fry until it starts to turn golden. Add the salami and warm through slightly. Add the white wine and continue cooking until it has evaporated. Skin, deseed, and cut the tomatoes into small cubes. Add them to the pan and cook on a moderate heat for 10 minutes. Cut the Provolone into thin strips and add to the pan with the tomatoes, stirring vigorously to amalgamate the sauce.
Cook the pasta in lightly salted boiling water and drain when *al dente*. Dress with the prepared sauce and sprinkled with the grated Parmigiano. Serve at once.

Italian Region: Campania.

ZITI E PATATE AL FORNO
BAKED ZITI WITH POTATO

Difficulty 2

Ingredients for 4 people
Preparation time: 1 h (preparation: 40' – cooking: 20')

9 oz (250 g) ziti
9 oz (250 g) potatoes
9 oz (250 g) fresh tomatoes
5 oz (150 g) pork sausage or salami
3 oz (80 g) Caciocavallo cheese

½ onion
1 green bell pepper
2 leaves basil
2 tbs (40 ml) extra virgin olive oil
Salt

Method

Wash, skin, seed, and then cut the tomatoes into pieces. Slice the onion finely. Wash the pepper, remove the seeds, and cut into chunks. Peel the potatoes and cut into ⅛ in (3 mm) thick slices.

Heat the oil in a skillet over a medium heat, add the onion and the tomatoes, and cook for about 5 minutes. Add the pepper and the basil torn up into pieces by hand, and continue cooking for about 8 minutes. Season with salt to taste. Slice the sausage and the Caciocavallo. Cook the pasta in lightly salted boiling water. Drain when *al dente* and dress with half of the prepared sauce.

Arrange a layer of potato slices in a large baking dish; cover with a little sauce and distribute over it some of the sausage and the cheese. Continue with a layer of pasta and then with more sauce, followed by more sausage and cheese.

Once all the ingredients have been used up, cook in a hot oven at 400°F (200°C) until the crust has turned golden brown.

Italian Region: Calabria.

EGG PASTA

The use of pasta in traditional Italian dishes goes back a very long way. However, differing climatic conditions resulted in the evolution of different species of wheat that eventually led to significant differences in both production and taste. Indeed, in the south, the cultivation of durum wheat as a crop led to the production of dried wheat semolina pasta, whereas in the Po Valley and the areas further north, the growing of wheat favored pastas made with eggs that were meant to be eaten fresh.

Scientists tell us that during cooking, the proteins of durum wheat semolina are bound together by water, forming a sort of meshed network that keeps the starches together to avoid creating a glutinous effect.

Pasta made with wheat flour, on the other hand, can "overcook" because it forms a glutinous mesh network that is too large, thereby allowing the starches (which constitute about 70 per cent of the dough) to escape. This makes the pasta sticky, but it also means that it retains a strong taste of flour. For this reason it became customary to add eggs to the dough. The proteins in eggs allow for increased protection of the starch's structure. Adding eggs provides an obvious difference in taste—perfectly balanced, of course, by seasonings—but their addition does also mean a shorter shelf life and the need for consumers to "eat fresh."

Egg pasta comes in a variety of sizes. To this day, more than other pasta types, it represents the rich tradition of the Italian regions. The ability of a housewife in the Italian countryside in the last century was often measured on her ability to "tirare la sfoglia," to "roll the dough" with skill. A little girl's first grown-up toy often consisted of a pastry board, a rolling pin, and a cutter.

Traditional instruments, in addition to the above, include the simple knife with which the pasta is cut to make *tagliatelle, fettuccine, tagliolini, maltagliati* (names that designate the thickness of the cut), and a serrated cutting wheel. These were used to create various shapes, from the flat strips of pastry from which we get *reginette, pappardelle, lasagne,* and the *rettangoli* which can then be cut to make *farfalle.* The most consistent shapes are the ones that you obtain from grated pasta, like those used in soups.

With *lasagne* and *cannelloni*, recipes have been taken from those used on high days and holidays, such as baked pasta dishes. They can be stuffed in a thousand different ways according to the Italian region from which they come: with meat, vegetables, cheeses and sausages, or mixed with béchamel sauce to create the soft basis of these rich and much-appreciated dishes.

Egg pasta is now also produced on an industrial scale using durum wheat semolina and then dried, thus permitting a long shelf life and a wide range of gastronomic uses.

EGG PASTA PREPARATION

Preparation time: 35 minutes
Ingredients: for each 4 oz (100 g) of flour 1 egg

Place the flour onto a pastry board and make a well. Break the eggs into the center of the well and with the fingers or the prongs of a fork begin to combine to form a dough. Work the dough well, kneading by pressing down with the edge of the palms until it is smooth. Cover the dough with a dishtowel or plastic wrap and leave to rest for 20 minutes before proceeding.
The resting time serves to "relax" the pasta, otherwise it would be too "nervous and tired" before rolling out.

BIGOLI CON SALSA D'ANATRA

BIGOLI WITH DUCK SAUCE

Difficulty 1

Ingredients for 4 people
Preparation time: 1 h (preparation: 20' – cooking: 40')

FOR THE PASTA
10 oz (300 g) flour
2 eggs
¼ cup (60 ml) water

FOR THE SAUCE
7 oz (200 g) duck liver and giblets
7 oz (200 g) duck meat
1¼ oz (30 g) butter
4 tsp (20 ml) extra virgin olive oil
1 cup (200 ml) vegetable stock

4 ripe tomatoes
1 medium onion
½ cup (100 ml) red wine
3 sprigs thyme
2 sprigs marjoram
1 bay leaf
2 oz (50 g) grated Parmigiano
1 spoonful parsley
Salt
Pepper

Method

Place the flour on a pastry board and make a well in the center. Break the eggs into this, add the water. Work all the ingredients and knead until you have a smooth dough. Cover the dough and leave to rest for about 20 minutes. Pass the dough through a suitable setting on a pasta machine or pass it through a mincing machine with a ⅛ in (3 mm) diameter hole. Chop the onion finely. Cut up the giblets, the liver, and the duck meat into very small little squares.

Place a skillet onto a medium heat with the butter and the oil, and when hot, add the onion. Sauté for a few minutes, just until it is nicely golden, but not too dark. Add the chopped giblets, liver, and duck meat; cook for 5 minutes or so, until brown. Pour in the red wine and cook to evaporate completely. Skin, seed, and roughly chop the tomatoes. Add the herbs, stripping the leaves carefully from the stems, the bay leaf, and finally the tomatoes. Cook for about 30 minutes, adding a little stock, a bit at a time, to avoid it drying out. Season with salt and pepper to taste.

In the meantime cook the bigoli pasta in a large pan of lightly salted boiling water until *al dente*. Drain the bigoli, place in a pan with the sauce, and toss. Remove from the heat and sprinkle the grated Parmigiano and the finely chopped parsley over the top. Arrange on a serving dish.

Chef's Tips

The chopped parsley should be added right at the end of cooking so that it does not wilt or lose its bright green color and distinctive flavor.

Italian Region: Veneto.

FOOD HISTORY

This traditional specialty from the Veneto is, in fact, one that goes all the way back to the eighteenth century. Bigoli, a hard wheat pasta, was originally made with a special "bigolaro," a wire press made of brass that produced the authentic bigolo shape—a sort of wrinkly, fat spaghetti that is very well suited for collecting the pasta sauce.

BIGOLI IN SALSA
BIGOLI WITH SARDINES

Difficulty 1

Ingredients for 4 people
Preparation time: 40' (preparation: 25' – cooking: 15')

FOR THE PASTA
10 oz (300 g) flour
2 eggs
3 cups (600 ml) water

FOR THE SAUCE
2 onions
2½ oz (60 g) salted sardines
2 tbs (30 ml) oil
Salt
Pepper

Method

Heap the flour on a pastry board and make a well in the center. Beat the eggs and add to the flour with the water. Knead until the dough is smooth. Cover the pasta and leave to rest for about 20 minutes. Pass the dough though a pasta machine on an appropriate setting or through a mincing machine with a ⅛ in (3 mm) diameter hole.

Thoroughly wash and clean the salted sardines. Cut them into small pieces and slice the onions. Heat the oil in a skillet over a medium heat, add the onions and the sardines, and sauté slowly. Add 4 tsp of water. When the onions are beginning to color, stir continuously for a few minutes to produce the "salsa."

Cook the bigoli in a pan of lightly salted boiling water and drain when *al dente*. Dress with the prepared sauce and drizzle over some olive oil. No other flavoring is added to this simple dish, which is traditionally popular because it is so economical and easy to prepare. There is a variant on this recipe: Substitute the onion with two or three cloves of crushed garlic. The dish will be even more flavorful, with a stronger taste.

Italian Region: Veneto.

BUSIATI COL PESTO TRAPANESE
BUSIATI WITH TRAPANI PESTO

Difficulty 1

Ingredients for 4 people
Preparation time: 45' (preparation: 40' – cooking: 5')

FOR THE PASTA
10 oz (300 g) flour
2 eggs
2½ cup (60 ml) olive oil

FOR THE SAUCE
14 oz (400 g) ripe tomatoes, skinned and seeded
2 cloves garlic
1½ oz (40 g) shelled almonds
1½ oz (40 g) breadcrumbs
2½ cup (60 ml) olive oil
5 leaves basil
salt
pepper

Method

Heap the flour on a board and make a well in the center. Break the eggs into the flour and add the oil. Work and knead until you have a smooth dough. In the Trapani area this pasta is known as "busiato" because, after having been put through a pasta machine, it is shaped into a sort of fusillo by being quickly rolled around a "busu" or knitting needle.

Blanch the almonds for a few moments in boiling water, then rub off the skins. Toast the almonds in the oven; chop them very finely.

In a pan of boiling water, blanch the tomatoes for 15–20 seconds. Remove the skins and seeds, and chop them into pieces. Then pulp the pieces in a mortar with salt, basil, pepper, and the clove of garlic. When it is well combined, add a little of the olive oil and the chopped almonds. Grease a skillet lightly with olive oil and toast the breadcrumbs.

Cook the busiati for 5 minutes in lightly salted boiling water, drain, and dress with the tomato and almond pesto. Arrange the pasta on a serving dish, sprinkle with the toasted breadcrumbs, and serve hot.

Italian Region: Sicily.

CHITARRINE ALL'UOVO CON PROSCIUTTO CRUDO
EGG CHITARRINE WITH PROSCIUTTO

Difficulty 2

Ingredients for 4 people
Preparation time: 15' (preparation: 10' – cooking: 5')

FOR THE PASTA
14 oz (400 g) flour
4 eggs

FOR THE SAUCE
4 oz (100 g) butter
5 oz (150 g) prosciutto
2 oz (50 g) grated Parmigiano
Salt

Method

Heap the flour on a board and make a well in the center. Break the eggs into the well. Knead until you have a smooth dough. Leave to rest for 20 minutes. Roll out the pasta to a fairly thin sheet. Flour lightly. Fold the pasta over onto itself several times and, with a knife, cut the chitarrine into ¼ in (5 mm) wide strips. Arrange the chitarrine to dry on a lightly floured tray in a well-aired room.

Cut the prosciutto into small strips. Place a pan onto a low heat, adding the butter. As soon as it has melted, combine with the prosciutto, making sure that it doesn't fry in the butter.
Cook the pasta in lightly salted boiling water and drain when *al dente*. Transfer to the pan with the butter and the prosciutto, add the Parmigiano. Combine well and serve.

FETTUCCINE ALLA CIOCIARA
FETTUCCINE WITH MEAT SAUCE

Difficulty 2

Ingredients for 4 people
Preparation time: 50' (preparation: 40' – cooking: 10')

FOR THE PASTA
14 oz (400 g) flour
4 eggs
2 tsp (10 ml) oil
Salt

FOR THE DRESSING
5 oz (150 g) butter
4 oz (100 g) meat sauce
4 oz (100 g) grated Pecorino

Method

Heap the flour on a board and make a well in the center. Break the eggs into the flour, add the oil and a pinch of salt. Work until the dough is smooth and velvety to the touch. Cover in plastic wrap and leave to rest for about 30 minutes. Roll out the pasta to a fairly thin sheet. Fold the sheet over onto itself several times, and cut into strips of just over ¼ in (5 mm). Arrange on a tray covered with a lightly floured clean cloth and leave to dry in a well-aired room.
Cook the fettuccine in a large pan of lightly salted boiling water. Drain when it is *al dente*. Arrange on a serving dish allowing the pasta to fully absorb the melted butter and the meat sauce. Sprinkle with a generous amount of grated Pecorino.

Italian Region: Lazio.

FETTUCCINE ALLA PIEMONTESE
PIEDMONT-STYLE FETTUCCINE

Difficulty 2

Ingredients for 4 people
Preparation time: 40' (preparation: 30' – cooking: 10')

PASTA
14 oz (400 g) flour
4 eggs
2 tsp (10 ml) extra virgin olive oil
¾ oz (20 g) grated Parmigiano
Water (if needed)

FOR THE DRESSING
1⅓ cup (300 ml) meat sauce
3 oz (80 g) butter
4 oz (100 g) grated Parmigiano
2½ oz (60 g) white truffle
Nutmeg
Salt
White pepper

Method

Heap the flour on a board and make a well in the center. Break the eggs into the flour. Knead until the dough is smooth. Leave to rest for 20 minutes.
Roll out the pasta dough to a fairly thin sheet and lightly flour. Fold the sheet over onto itself several times and, with a knife, cut into strips of fettuccine about a ½ in (10 mm) wide. Lay them out on a lightly floured tray to dry in a well-aired room.

Place a large pan onto a low heat and warm the meat sauce through.

Cook the pasta in lightly salted boiling water and drain when *al dente*. Coat with the butter, half the grated Parmigiano, some ground white pepper, a dusting of nutmeg, and shavings of truffle.

Serve accompanied with the rest of the Parmigiano and the meat sauce.

Italian Region: Piedmont.

FETTUCCINE ALLA ROMANA
ROMAN-STYLE FETTUCCINE

Difficulty 2

Ingredients for 4 people
Preparation time: 1 h 5' (preparation: 35' – cooking: 30')

FOR THE PASTA
14 oz (400 g) flour
4 eggs

FOR THE DRESSING
½ cup (100 ml) meat sauce
2 oz (50 g) lard
1 onion
4 oz (100 g) chicken giblets

7 oz (200 g) chicken
2 oz (50 g) dried mushrooms
¼ cup (50 ml) tomato sauce
½ cup (100 ml) stock
1¼ oz (30 g) butter
2 oz (50 g) grated Pecorino
Salt
Pepper

Method

Heap the flour on a pastry board and make a well in the center. Break the eggs into it and work into a dough. Knead until smooth and velvety to the touch. Wrap in plastic wrap and allow to rest for 30 minutes. Roll out the dough and cut into strips about ¼ in (5mm) wide. Place the fettuccine to dry on a lightly floured tray. Soak the mushrooms in water. Chop the onion. Dice the giblets and the chicken into very small pieces.

Drain and roughly chop the mushrooms. Place a skillet onto a medium heat with the lard and when melted, add the onion and cook for a few minutes until it starts to color. Add the mushrooms and sauté until golden. Add the meat and cook for about 5 minutes, until nicely browned. Pour in the tomato sauce and simmer over a low heat for around 20 minutes, adding stock so it does not dry out. Season with salt and pepper to taste.

Cook the fettuccine in a large pan of lightly salted boiling and drain when *al dente*. Dress with the meat sauce and place in an ovenproof dish, covering it with the prepared ragù and the grated Pecorino.

Italian Region: Lazio.

FETTUCCINE CON FUNGHI
FETTUCCINE WITH MUSHROOMS

Difficulty 1

Ingredients for 4 people
Preparation time: 50' (preparation: 40' – cooking: 10')

FOR THE PASTA
14 oz (400 g) flour
4 eggs

FOR THE SAUCE
10 oz (300 g) button mushrooms
4 oz (100 g) prosciutto
3 oz (80 g) butter
3 or 4 leaves basil
1½ oz (40 g) Parmigiano
Salt

Method

Heap the flour on a board and make a well in the center. Break in the eggs. Knead until the dough is smooth. Leave to rest for 20 minutes. Roll out into a fairly thin sheet of pasta and lightly flour. Fold the pasta over onto itself several times and, with a knife, cut into strips of fettuccine about ¼ in (5 mm) wide. Lay the fettuccine out on a lightly floured tray and leave to dry in a well-aired room.

Clean the mushrooms, removing any soil with a brush or a damp cloth. Cut the prosciutto into small strips.

Place a pan onto a medium heat and add two-thirds of the butter. When melted and just getting hot, add the mushrooms. Cook over a high heat for 3–4 minutes, then add the prosciutto and the basil leaves, which have been torn up into pieces by hand.
Stir well, season with salt, and remove the pan immediately from the stove.

Cook the fettuccine in a pan of lightly salted boiling water and drain when *al dente*. Coat with the prepared sauce, adding the rest of the butter and the grated Parmigiano. If the fettuccine seem a bit dry, add a little of the cooking water with the sauce.

FETTUCCINE IN TIMBALLO
FETTUCCINE IN TIMBALLO

Difficulty 2

Ingredients for 4 people
Preparation time: 55' (preparation: 45 – cooking: 10')

FOR THE PASTA
14 oz (400 g) flour
4 eggs

FOR THE SAUCE
7 oz (200 g) butter
24 salted anchovies
3 oz (75 g) grated Parmigiano
3 oz (75 g) Gruyère
5 oz (150 g) mozzarella
Salt
White pepper

Method

Heap the flour on a board and make a well in the center. Break the eggs into the flour. Knead until the dough is smooth. Leave to rest for 20 minutes.

Roll out the dough to a sheet of fairly thin pasta. Lightly flour and then fold it over on itself several times. With a knife cut out the fettuccine into ¼ in (5 mm) strips. Lay out the fettuccine on a lightly floured tray in a well-aired room to dry.

Rinse and bone the anchovies and cut up into small pieces.
Cube the mozzarella.
Place a pan onto a low heat and warm through 5 oz (150 g) of butter. When it starts to get hot, add half of the anchovies and, keeping the heat low, stir with a wooden spoon until they have softened into a pulp.
Cook the fettuccine in a pan of boiling water and drain when *al dente*. Coat with the prepared anchovy sauce. It is best not to add salt to the water in which the pasta is cooked as the anchovy sauce is already fairly salty. Grate the Gruyère.

Dress the pasta with the rest of the Parmigiano and half the Gruyère. Lightly butter a fairly shallow ovenproof dish and fill with a generous half of the dressed fettuccine. Follow with the mozzarella, the remaining anchovies, and a pinch of white pepper. Cover with the rest of the pasta, carefully piling it up to give the timballo a dome shape. Finally sprinkle over the reserved Parmigiano and Gruyere, with pats of butter dotted here and there. Place the timballo into a hot oven for about 10 minutes or until nicely browned. Serve piping hot.

GARGANELLI CON PROSCIUTTO E PISELLI
GARGANELLI WITH PROSCIUTTO AND PEAS

Difficulty 1

Ingredients for 4 people
Preparation time: 45' (preparation: 30' – cooking: 15')

10½ oz (320 g) garganelli
5 oz (150 g) prosciutto
9 oz (250 g) frozen or fresh peas
1 onion
7 oz (200 g) butter
5 oz (150 g) grated Parmigiano
Salt
White pepper

Method

Place a skillet over a low heat with half the butter. Add the chopped onion and sauté gently without allowing it to color. Stir in the peas and season with salt and ground white pepper. Add a few spoonfuls of water and turn up the heat to cook the peas. Cut the prosciutto into strips and add before the peas are completely cooked.

Cook the pasta in lightly salted boiling water and drain when *al dente*. Dress with the prepared sauce, add the remaining butter and half of the Parmigiano. Stir together carefully and bring to the table with the remaining Parmigiano served separately.

LANCETTE - PASTA E FAGIOLI
LANCETTE AND BEAN SOUP

Difficulty 2

Ingredients for 4 people
Preparation time: 1 h 25' (preparation: 15' – cooking: 1 h 10')

9 oz (250 g) lancette
1 lb 2 oz (500 g) fresh borlotti beans
4 oz (100 g) onion
7 oz (200 g) red potatoes
5 oz (150 g) lard
10½ cups (2.5 l) meat stock
1 sprig rosemary

1 tbs chopped parsley
2 oz (50 g) grated Parmigiano
2 slices bread
1 clove garlic
Salt
Pepper

Method

Peel the potatoes. Chop finely the lard, the rosemary, and the onion. Heat one third of the oil in a skillet over a medium heat, add the onion and the lard, and cook until the onion starts to brown. Add the beans and the stock, followed by the potato, and simmer for about an hour on a medium heat. When the beans are cooked, take out about one-third. Drain the potatoes, pass them both through a sieve, then return the purée back to the pan.

Bring back to the boil and add the pasta. Cook until *al dente*. Finish with a generous amount of grated Parmigiano and the rest of the olive oil. Serve in individual bowls with slices of toasted bread, rubbed with the garlic.

Italian Region: Piedmont.

MALTAGLIATI FRESCHI - PASTA E CECI

PASTA WITH GARBANZO

Difficulty 2

Ingredients for 4 people

Preparation time: 2 h (12 hours for soaking the garbanzo beans) (preparation: 30' – cooking: 1 h 30')

FOR THE PASTA
7 oz (200 g) flour
2 eggs

FOR THE SAUCE
10 oz (300 g) garbanzo beans
1 clove garlic

4 oz (100 g) lard
2 tbs (40 ml) extra virgin olive oil
1 sprig rosemary
2 oz (50 g) grated Parmigiano
1½ oz (40 g) tomato paste
Salt
Pepper

Method

Place the garbanzo beans into a bowl of cold water to soak for 12 hours.
Heap the flour on a board and make a well in the center. Break the eggs into the flour.
Knead until the dough is smooth. Leave to rest for 20 minutes.
Roll the dough out to a fairly thin sheet of pasta and lightly flour. Fold the pasta over on to itself several times and, with a knife, cut the fettuccine into strips of about ½ in (10 mm). Lay them out on a lightly floured tray in a well-aired room and leave to dry.
Cut the fettuccine with a knife or by hand so you have pieces of pasta about ¾ in (2 cm) long. Finely chop the lard, the garlic, and the rosemary. Place a pan onto a medium heat, add one-third of the oil, the garlic and the lard; fry until lightly brown. Add the tomato paste, the chickpeas, and 10½ cups (2.5 l) of warm water. When the garbanzi are cooked (around 1 hour) remove half and pass them through a sieve. Return the purée to the pan.
Bring back to the boil, add the maltagliati, and cook until al dente. Serve hot with plenty of grated Parmigiano and the remaining extra virgin olive oil.

Italian Region: Umbria.

MALTAGLIATI CON I FAGIOLI
MALTAGLIATI SOUP WITH BEANS

Difficulty 1

Ingredients for 4 people
Preparation time: 1 h 5' (12 hours for soaking the beans) (preparation: 15' – cooking: 50')

FOR THE PASTA
10 oz (300 g) flour
3 eggs

FOR THE SOUP
10 oz (300 g) borlotti beans
9 oz (250 g) pork rinds/pork crunch
2 oz (50 g) fat of prosciutto
3 oz (80 g) onion
Ham bone
Cinnamon powder
1¼ oz (30 g) extra virgin olive oil
Water
Salt
Pepper

Method

Place the borlotti beans to soak in cold water for 12 hours with a pinch of baking soda to help soften the beans.

Heap the flour on a board, make a well in the center, and add the eggs. Knead until the dough is smooth. Leave to rest for 20 minutes.
Roll out the pasta to a fairly thin sheet and lightly flour. Fold the pasta on top of itself several times and, with a knife, cut the fettuccine into about ½ in (10 mm) strips. Arrange the maltagliati on a lightly floured pastry board to dry in a well-aired room.
Boil the ham bone and the pork rind for 10 minutes. Take the rinds and scrape them, holding over a flame (to help to thoroughly clean the skins). Wash them in cold water, then cut up into small pieces. Remove from the bone the parts that will not be used. Finely chop the prosciutto fat and the onion.
Heat the oil in a skillet over a medium heat. Add the onion, the fat from the prosciutto, the rinds, the bone; add the borlotti beans; then season with the cinnamon and the ground pepper. Cover with plenty of water, cover, and cook over a low heat. When the borlotti beans are ready, remove the ham bone and break it up with a meat cleaver, extracting the bone marrow. Return to the pan. Drain half the borlotti beans and pass through a sieve; then return to the pan.

Bring back to the boil and adjust the seasoning. Break up the pasta into 5 cm pieces and cook them in the soup. Once *al dente*, remove the pan from the heat. Leave to rest for a couple of minutes and serve.

Italian Region: Emilia-Romagna.

MINESTRA DI FAGIOLI CON PASTA ALLA VENETA
MINESTRA SOUP WITH VENETIAN-STYLE BORLOTTI BEANS

Difficulty 2

Ingredients for 4 people
Preparation time: 2 h 10'
(12 hours for soaking the beans) (preparation: 40' – cooking: 1 h 30')

FOR THE PASTA
10 oz (300 g) flour
3 eggs

FOR THE SOUP
10 oz (300 g) borlotti beans
9 oz (250 g) pork rinds/pork crunch
2 oz (50 g) fat of prosciutto

3 oz (80 g) onion
Ham bone
Cinnamon powder
1¼ oz (30 g) extra virgin olive oil
Water
Salt
Pepper

Method

Place the borlotti beans to soak in cold water for 12 hours with a pinch of baking soda to help soften the beans.

Heap the flour on a board, make a well in the center, and add the eggs. Knead until the dough is smooth. Leave to rest for 20 minutes.

Roll out the pasta to a fairly thin sheet and lightly flour. Fold the pasta on top of itself several times and, with a knife, cut the fettuccine into about ½ in (10 mm) strips. Arrange the fettuccine on a lightly floured pastry board to dry in a well-aired room.

Boil the ham bone and the pork rind for 10 minutes. Take the rinds and scrape them, holding over a flame (to help to thoroughly clean the skins). Wash them in cold water, then cut up into small pieces. Remove from the bone the parts that will not be used. Finely chop the prosciutto fat and the onion.

Heat the oil in a skillet over a medium heat. Add the onion, the fat from the prosciutto, the rinds, the bone; add the borlotti beans; then season with the cinnamon and the ground pepper.

Cover with plenty of water, cover, and cook over a low heat.

When the borlotti beans are ready, remove the ham bone and break it up with a meat cleaver, extracting the bone marrow. Return to the pan. Drain half the borlotti beans and pass through a sieve; then return to the pan.

Bring back to the boil and adjust the seasoning.

Break up the pasta into 5 cm pieces and cook them in the soup. Once *al dente*, remove the pan from the heat.

Leave to rest for a couple of minutes and serve.

Italian Region: Veneto.

MINESTRA DI TAGLIOLINI
TAGLIOLINI SOUP

Difficulty 1

Ingredients for 4 people
Preparation time: 33' (preparation: 30' – cooking: 3')

FOR THE PASTA
14 oz (400 g) flour
4 eggs
1¼ oz (30 g) grated Parmigiano
Nutmeg
8½ cups (2 l) meat stock
Salt

Method

Heap the flour on a board and make a well in the center. Break the eggs into the flour, add the Parmigiano and a pinch of nutmeg. Knead until the dough is smooth. Leave to rest for 20 minutes.
Roll the dough out to a fairly thin sheet of pasta and lightly flour. Fold the sheet over onto itself several times and, with a knife, cut the tagliolini into about ¾ in (20 mm) lengths. Lay the tagliolini onto a lightly floured tray in a well-aired room and leave to dry.

Bring the stock to the boil in a pan and cook the tagliolini for 2 minutes. Serve at once.

PAGLIA E FIENO ALLO ZAFFERANO
PAGLIA E FIENO WITH SAFFRON

Difficulty 1

Ingredients for 4 people
Preparation time: 15' (preparation: 5 – cooking: 10')

10½ oz (320 g) tagliatelle "paglia and fieno"
1 pack Saffron
1 shallot
¼ oz (10 g) fresh cream
1½ oz (40 g) butter
2 oz (50 g) grated Parmigiano
Salt
Pepper

Method

Finely chop the shallot. Place a skillet onto a medium heat, add the butter and, when hot, add the shallot and fry slowly. Dissolve the saffron in a small glass of warm water. When the shallot has softened, add the cream and the saffron with the water.

Finely chop the shallot. Place a skillet onto a medium heat, add the butter and, when hot, add the shallot and fry slowly. Dissolve the saffron in a small glass of warm water. When the shallot has softened, add the cream and the saffron with the water.

PAPPARDELLE AL SUGO DI LEPRE
PAPPARDELLE WITH HARE SAUCE

Difficulty 2

Ingredients for 4 people
Preparation time: 2 h' 30' (preparation: 30' – cooking: 2 h)

FOR THE PASTA
14 oz (400 g) flour
4 eggs

FOR THE SAUCE
14 oz (400 g) hare
1½ oz (40 g) carrot
1½ oz (40 g) onion
1½ oz (40 g) celery
½ cup (100 ml) red wine
½ cup (100 ml) milk
2 oz (50 g) tomato sauce
1½ oz (40 g) extra virgin olive oil
2 oz (50 g) grated Parmigiano
Salt
Pepper

Method

Heap the flour on a board and make a well in the center. Break the eggs into the flour. Knead until the dough is smooth. Leave to rest for 20 minutes.

Roll out the dough to a fairly thin sheet and lightly flour. Fold the pasta over onto itself several times and, with a knife, cut the pappardelle into ¾ in (20 mm) strips. Lay out the pappardelle on a lightly floured tray and leave to dry in a well-aired room.
Finely chop the carrot, the onion, and the celery.

Cut the hare meat into pieces. Warm on the stove a large pot, preferably a crock-pot, and add the oil. Sauté the vegetables and when they have softened and are starting to color, add the hare meat and cook until well browned. Remove the pieces of hare from the pan, chop up quite small, and then return to the heat, cooking for a further 5 minutes.
Cook the pasta in boiling water, drain when *al dente*, and dress with the prepared sauce. Sprinkle over the grated Parmigiano and serve at once.

Italian Region: Tuscany.

PASSATELLI

PASSATELLI

Difficulty 1

Ingredients for 4 people
Preparation time: 35' (preparation: 30' – cooking: 5')

9 oz (250 g) grated Parmigiano
7 oz (200 g) breadcrumbs
¾ oz (20 g) butter
1½ oz (35 g) flour

4 eggs
8½ cups (2 l) stock
Nutmeg
Salt

Method

Work the eggs, the breadcrumbs, 5 oz (150 g) of the Parmigiano, the butter, the flour, salt, pepper, and nutmeg together to form a dough. Cover with plastic wrap and leave to rest for 20 minutes. In a pan, bring the stock (preferably chicken stock made with a capon) to the boil. With the aid of a potato ricer—in the absence of a special "iron" with a disk featuring larger holes—pass through all the mixture to obtain strips the length of a finger. Drop the passatelli straight into the boiling stock. Cook thoroughly and serve in soup bowls with the stock and a generous helping of grated Parmigiano.

Italian Region: Emilia-Romagna.

FOOD HISTORY

One of the most highly rated spices in traditional Italian cuisine is nutmeg, the seed of the fruit of the myrustica fragrans, an evergreen tree originally from an atoll in the Pacific Ocean, and cultivated in different areas along the equator.
Until a century ago, nutmeg was one of the rarest and most precious spices in the world. At one time, the nutmeg tree only grew on the slopes of the Run volcano in the Spice, or Maluku Islands. The journey to reach the islands was an extremely difficult and dangerous one, yet, from 1500, the major European powers embarked on a race against each other in search of this precious spice. The conditions were so treacherous that two out of three of the ships did not return, and even those that were successful in their undertaking came back decimated. Despite this, Holland, Britain, and Portugal were drawn into a bitter contest for control of the nutmeg market, a spice which, at the time, was even more highly prized for its gastronomical uses than for its presumed aphrodisiacal and medicinal powers: It was considered to be a cure for the plague. The three great European powers were engaged in a long drawn battle which only came to an end when Holland appeared to succeed in getting the better of both the Portuguese, who effectively withdrew from the fight to concentrate their efforts in their South American colonies, and the British. The Dutch and the British came to an accord whereby the Dutch would have the exclusive rights to the sale of nutmeg from Run and, in exchange, the British would be given a small island in North America that the Duke of York had illegally occupied for a number of years. At the signing of the agreement, the Dutch were convinced that they had struck a brilliant deal, but in quite a short time the British had managed to cultivate the myrustica fragrans tree elsewhere, depriving the Dutch of their monopoly, while the little island given to the British was none other than Manhattan.

SPAGHETTI ALLA CHITARRA
SPAGHETTI ALLA CHITARRA

Difficulty 2

Ingredients for 4 people
Preparation time: 52' (preparation: 40' – cooking: 12')

FOR THE PASTA
14 oz (400 g) durum wheat flour
4 eggs

FOR THE SAUCE
¼ cup (60 ml) extra virgin olive oil
4 oz (100 g) veal
2 oz (50 g) pork
2 oz (50 g) mutton
¼ cup (50 ml) eed wine
14 oz (400 g) tomato sauce
2½ oz (60 g) grated Pecorino
1 dried chilli
Salt

Method

Roll out the pasta dough to a ⅛ in (3 mm) thick sheet. Cut the sheet into strips as wide as the width of the "chitarra," the pasta-cutting tool. Rest the floured strips on the "chitarra" and pass the rolling pin over the pasta with a pressing rather than a stretching movement. This way the pasta will be cut and separated by the steel wires. Lay out the pasta on a lightly floured tray to dry. Heat the oil in a large skillet over a medium heat and, when hot, add the chopped onion and cook until soft. Turn up the heat and add the ground veal and pork. Sauté until nicely browned. Add the wine and continue cooking until the liquid has completely evaporated. Add the tomato sauce and cook for around 15 minutes. Season with salt and add the crushed dried chilli. Cook the pasta in lightly salted boiling water and drain when *al dente*. Dress with the prepared sauce and the grated Pecorino; serve.

Chitarra abruzzese (in dialect "carrature"), or the Abruzzo guitar, is the name given not just to the pasta but also to the characteristic rectangular wooden frame with its many steel wires, placed just over 1mm apart. With all its keys to hold the wires taut and on which to drop the pasta, this in its simplicity and perfection is the instrument that gives life to the pasta that is a cross-section of the typical spaghetti.

Italian Region: Abruzzo.

SPAGHETTI ALLA CHITARRA
CON ERBE AROMATICHE E PECORINO

SPAGHETTI ALLA CHITARRA WITH HERBS AND PECORINO

Difficulty 1

Ingredients for 4 people
Preparation time: 15' (preparation: 10' – cooking: 5')

10½ oz (320 g) spaghetti alla chitarra
¼ cup (50 ml) extra virgin olive oil
½ spoonful chopped mint
½ spoonful chopped marjoram
½ spoonful scallion
1 tsp chopped rosemary
1 spoonful chopped parsley
1 spoonful chopped basil
2 cloves chopped garlic
2½ oz (60 g) grated Pecorino
¾ oz (20 g) shavings
½ oz (15 g) butter
Salt
Pepper

Method

Place a medium-sized skillet onto a low heat. Warm the oil with the aromatic herbs and the chopped garlic, and sauté gently to soften for 2–3 minutes. Add a generous amount of pepper. Cook the pasta in lightly salted boiling water and drain when *al dente*. Dress with the prepared sauce, adding the grated Pecorino and the butter. Stir well together and serve garnished with the Pecorino shavings.

TAGLIATELLE AL RAGÙ
TAGLIATELLE WITH BOLOGNESE SAUCE

Difficulty 2

Ingredients for 4 people
Preparation time: 40' (preparation: 30' – cooking: 10')

FOR THE PASTA:
14 oz (400 g) flour
4 eggs

FOR DRESSING
14 oz (400 g) bolognese sauce
2½ oz (60 g) grated Parmigiano

Method

Heap the flour on a board and make a well in the center. Break the eggs into the flour. Knead until the dough is smooth. Leave to rest for 20 minutes.

Roll out the pasta dough to a fairly thin sheet and flour lightly. Fold the sheet over onto itself several times and, with a knife, cut into strips of tagliatelle about ¼ in (5 mm) wide. Lay out the tagliatelle on a lightly floured tray and leave to dry in a well-aired room.

Place a large pan onto a low heat and warm through the ragù bolognese Cook the pasta in lightly salted boiling water, drain when *al dente*, and dress with the ragù. Sprinkle with the grated Parmigiano and serve.

Italian Region: Emilia-Romagna.

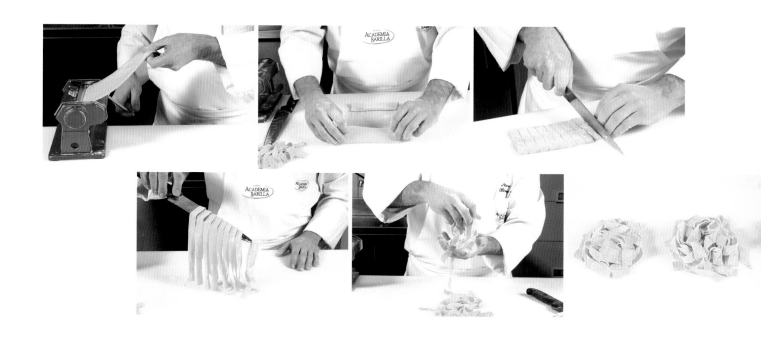

TAGLIATELLE AL TARTUFO
TAGLIATELLE WITH TRUFFLE

Difficulty 2

Ingredients for 4 people
Preparation time: 35' (preparation: 30' – cooking: 5')

FOR THE PASTA
14 oz (400 g) flour
4 eggs

FOR THE DRESSING
1½ oz (40 g) grated Parmigiano
4 oz (100 g) butter

1 clove garlic
3 leaves sage
½ stock cube
2 oz (50 g) truffle
Salt
Pepper

Method

Heap the flour on a board and make a well in the center. Break the eggs into the flour. Knead until the dough is smooth. Leave to rest for 20 minutes.
Roll out the pasta dough to fairly thin sheet and flour lightly. Fold the sheet over onto itself several times and, with a knife, cut into strips of tagliatelle of about ¼ in (5 mm) wide. Lay out the pasta on a lightly floured tray and leave to dry in a well-aired room.

Place a pan onto a medium heat and gently heat in the butter the clove of garlic and the sage leaves torn up by hand. Add half a stock cube and a ladle of water; reduce to a low heat. Add the Parmigiano and adjust the seasoning.
Cook the pasta in lightly salted boiling water and drain when *al dente*. Dress with the previously prepared sauce. Cover with truffle shavings and serve.

Italian Region: Piedmont.

TAGLIATELLE CON BORRAGINI
TAGLIATELLE WITH BORAGE

Difficulty 2

Ingredients for 4 people
Preparation time: 45' (preparation: 30' – cooking: 15')

FOR THE PASTA
10 oz (300 g) flour
4 oz (100 g) borage
3 egg yolks
¼ oz (10 g) grated Parmigiano

FOR THE DRESSING
4 oz (100 g) button mushrooms
2 oz (50 g) butter
1½ oz (40 g) grated Parmigiano
Salt
Pepper

Method

Heap the flour on a board, make a well in the center, and add the eggs. Knead until the dough is smooth. Leave to rest for 20 minutes.
Place a pan of water onto the stove. When it boils, add the borage. Cook, drain, and squeeze out any excess water. Chop up very finely.
Incorporate the borage into the dough with the Parmigiano. Cover the pasta in plastic wrap and leave to rest for about 20 minutes. Roll out the pasta to a fairly thin sheet and lightly flour. Fold the pasta over onto itself several times and, with a knife, cut the tagliatelle into about ¼ in (5mm) wide strips. Place the tagliatelle on a lightly floured tray to dry out in a well-aired room.

Cut the mushrooms into very thin slices. Place a pan onto a medium heat, add the butter and, when it has melted, add the mushrooms. Cook for 5 minutes, then season with salt and pepper.
Cook the tagliatelle in lightly salted boiling water. Drain when *al dente* and dress with the prepared mushroom sauce. Sprinkle with the grated Parmigiano and serve.

Italian Region: Liguria.

TAGLIATELLE IN PASTICCIO
TAGLIATELLE PIE

Difficulty 2

Ingredients for 4 people
Preparation time: 1 h 10' (preparation: 30' – cooking: 40')

4 oz (400g) egg tagliatelle

FOR THE BRISÉ PASTRY
14 oz (400 g) flour
7 oz (200 g) butter
2 whole eggs
2 egg yolks
¼ cup (50 ml) dry white wine

FOR THE DRESSING
5 oz (150 g) cream
2½ oz (60 g) grated Parmigiano
2 oz (50 g) butter
Salt

Method

Place the flour in a heap on a pastry board and make a hollow in the center. Break two eggs into this plus one egg yolk. Add 5 oz (150 g) of the butter, which has been left to soften at room temperature, and the white wine. Combine all the ingredients and work to obtain a smooth dough.

Cover and leave the dough to rest in a cool place for about 30 minutes.

In the meantime, cook the tagliatelle in a large pan of lightly salted boiling water until *al dente*. Melt 1oz (25g) butter in a skillet and add to it the well-drained tagliatelle.

Mix together 3 tbs of the pasta-cooking water, the cream, the rest of the butter, and the grated Parmigiano. Toss all together for a few seconds over a medium heat.

In the meantime, roll out the brisé pastry to form two discs, 3mm thick; make one a bit larger. Grease a deep pie dish with the remaining butter, then it with the larger disc. Transfer the cooked tagliatelle to the mold and cover with the smaller disc, sealing all the edges.
Beat the remaining egg yolk with a spoonful of water and use this to brush the pie surface. Bake in the oven at 360°F (180°C) for 30 minutes. Remove, leave to rest for 5 minutes, and serve.

Italian Region: Emilia-Romagna.

TAGLIERINI PASTICCIATI ALL'ITALIANA
ITALIAN-STYLE TAGLIERINI PIE

Difficulty 2

Ingredients for 4 people
Preparation time: 55′ (preparation: 40′ – cooking: 15′)

FOR THE PASTA
14 oz (400 g) flour
4 eggs

FOR THE DRESSING
9 oz (250 g) meat sauce
2 tsp (10 ml) extra virgin olive oil
5 oz (150 g) chicken livers
2½ oz (60 g) butter
½ cup (100 ml) marsala wine
2½ oz (60 g) black truffle
4 oz (100 g) grated Parmigiano
Salt
Pepper

Method

Heap the flour on a board and make a well in the center. Break the eggs into the flour. Knead until the dough is smooth. Leave to rest for 20 minutes.
Roll out the pasta dough to a thin sheet and flour lightly. Fold the sheet over onto itself several times and, with a knife, cut into strips of tagliolini of about ⅛ in (3 mm) in width. Lay out on a lightly floured tray and leave to dry.

Place a large pan onto a high heat and add ¾ oz (20 g) of butter and the oil. When quite hot, add the chicken livers and stir-fry for 5 minutes. Season with salt and pepper to taste. Douse with the Marsala and simmer until completely evaporated. Combine with the meat sauce and continue cooking for another 5 minutes.

Place the pasta in lightly salted boiling water and drain 3–4 minutes after the water has come back to the boil. Dress with the prepared sauce. Butter an ovenproof dish with ¾ oz (20 g) of butter, place in it the dressed tagliolini and sprinkle with shavings of truffle, the rest of the melted butter, and plenty of Parmigiano. Put the dish into the oven and remove when well browned on top. Serve with the remaining Parmigiano on the side.

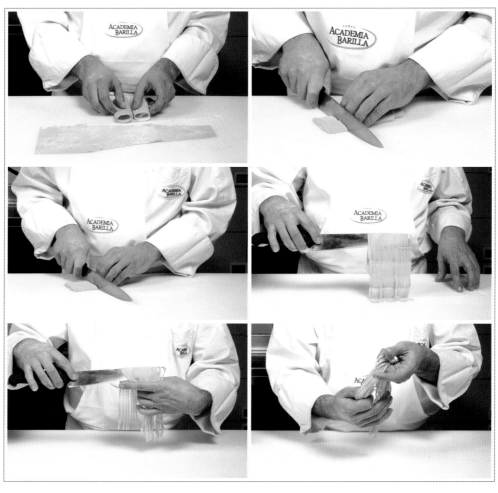

TAGLIOLINI AL TARTUFO NERO DI NORCIA
TAGLIOLINI WITH NORCIA BLACK TRUFFLES

Difficulty 2

Ingredients for 4 people
Preparation time: 45' (preparation: 40' – cooking: 5')

FOR THE PASTA
14 oz (400 g) flour
4 eggs

FOR THE DRESSING
¼ cup (50 ml) extra virgin olive oil
1 clove garlic
2 oz (50 g) black truffle
Salt

Method

Heap the flour on a board and make a well in the center. Break the eggs into the flour. Knead until the dough is smooth. Leave to rest for 20 minutes.
Roll out the pasta dough to a thin sheet and lightly flour. Fold the sheet over onto itself several times and, with a knife, cut into strips of tagliolini of about ⅛ in (3 mm) in width. Lay them out on a lightly floured tray and leave to dry. Heat the oil in a skillet over a low heat, add the garlic, and warm through without allowing it to color. Cook the pasta in lightly salted boiling water. Drain when *al dente*. Transfer to the skillet, add the truffle, cut into shavings, and toss everything together to bring out its full flavor.

Italian Region: Umbria.

TORCHIETTI E CECI CON PEPERONI SECCHI
TORCHIETTI WITH GARBANZO AND DRIED PEPPERS

Difficulty 1

Ingredients for 4 people
Preparation time: 1 h (preparation: 30' – cooking: 30')

FOR THE PASTA
10½ oz (320 g) flour
4 eggs
7 oz (200 g) garbanzo beans
2 bay leaves
5 sundried bell peppers in extra virgin olive oil
2 tbs (30 ml) extra virgin olive oil
Salt
Pepper

Method

Heap the flour on a board and make a well in the center. Break the eggs into the flour. Knead until the dough is smooth. Leave to rest for 20 minutes.

Roll out the dough to a fairly thin sheet and lightly flour. Fold over the pasta onto itself several times and, with a knife, cut the torchietti into strips about ¼ in (5 mm) wide. Arrange the torchietti on a lightly floured tray and leave to dry in a well-aired room. Soak the garbanzo beans overnight in plenty of water.

Place a terracotta pot onto the stove with the drained garbanzo beans and add 10½ cups (2.5 l) of water, salt, and the bay leaves. Simmer until the beans are soft (but not too soft and mushy), adding more water during cooking if necessary. Blend in the food processor one quarter of the cooked beans and season with salt and pepper to taste.

Cook the torchietti in lightly salted boiling water. Drain when *al dente* and add to the garbanzo beans. Place a small skillet onto heat, adding the oil and the drained bell peppers cut into small strips. When warm, scatter over the torchietti and serve.

Italian Region: Calabria.

FILLED PASTA

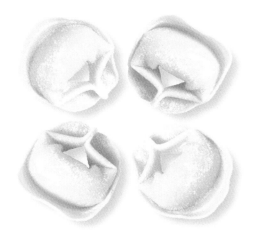

THE TRADITION OF PREPARING PASTA DISHES USING SOFT WHEAT FLOUR IS VERY OLD INDEED. THE ROMANS CULTIVATED IT THROUGHOUT THE PO VALLEY, IN CONTRAST TO THE DURUM WHEAT GROWN IN PUGLIA, SICILY, AND ALSO IN LIBYA. THE DIFFERENCES BETWEEN THE FLOURS GROWN IN THE TWO REGIONS RESULTED IN THE TRADITION OF FRESH PASTA—WHICH WAS OFTEN FILLED—IN THE NORTH AND DRIED PASTA IN THE SOUTH. AS EARLY AS THE FOURTH CENTURY BC, THE ETRUSCANS KNEW HOW TO MAKE DOUGH. IN TOMB RELIEFS AT THE CERVETERI NECROPOLIS, MIXING TOOLS SIMILAR TO THOSE USED TODAY CAN BE SEEN AND A FORERUNNER OF FILLED PASTA IS EVEN MENTIONED BY THE GREEK PLAYWRIGHT ARISTOPHANES, WHO SPEAKS IN THE FIFTH CENTURY AD OF A FILLING CONTAINED IN A PASTA CASE. THE ROMANS LEARNED THE ART OF PASTA-MAKING, LIKE MANY OTHER DIETARY PRACTICES, FROM THE GREEKS THROUGH THE MEDIATION OF THE SOUTHERN CITIES OF MAGNA GRAECIA ("GREATER GREECE"—THE COASTAL AREAS OF SOUTHERN ITALY SURROUNDING THE GULF OF TARANTO). IN HIS TREATISE *ON AGRICULTURE* IN THE SECOND CENTURY BC, CATO ADVISES HOUSEWIVES TO KNEAD THE DOUGH WELL, TO WORK IT WITH THEIR HANDS, FLATTENING AND SMOOTHING IT BEFORE DRYING IT ON A RACK. THE RICH MAN TRIMALCHIO DESCRIBED IN PETRONIUS' *SATYRICON* SERVES HIS PRECIOUS PASTA LAYERED WITH SEASONED *GARUM*, A FERMENTED FISH SAUCE MIXED WITH SPICES, DURING ONE OF HIS MANY PARTIES. THROUGHOUT THE MIDDLE AGES, TOO, THERE IS EVIDENCE OF FILLED PASTAS; IN PARMA'S *CHRONICA*, FRIAR SALIMBENE SPEAKS OF LASAGNA AND RAVIOLI. THE TRADITION OF STUFFED PASTA DURING THE RENAISSANCE ACQUIRED A GENUINE "REBIRTH" OF ITS OWN, WITH A SPECTACULAR SERIES OF VARIATIONS AND INVENTIONS, SOME OF WHICH ARE USED BY COURT KITCHENS TO THIS DAY.

AS SUCH, A FOOD PROCESS, INITIALLY BORNE OUT OF NEED AND NECESSITY, CAME TO BE USED TO FEED THE FAMILY. THANKS TO ITS VERSATILITY THERE WAS VERY LITTLE WASTE. OVER TIME IT EVEN WENT BEYOND THAT AS FILLED PASTA BECAME INCREASINGLY LINKED TO FEAST DAYS, ULTIMATELY BECOMING A SYMBOL OF PLENTY AND *JOIE DE VIVRE*. ALL FRESH PASTAS ARE TRADITIONAL DISHES WHICH VARY FROM REGION TO REGION; THEY ALL USE MIXTURES OF WHEAT-FLOUR DOUGH MADE WITH EGGS, KNEADED AND FILLED WITH DIFFERENT INGREDIENTS: CHEESE, MEAT, VEGETABLES, BLENDED INTO TASTY AND VARIED PREPARATIONS. THESE RECIPES ARE STUFFED TO MAKE THE DIFFERENT TYPES OF FILLED PASTA; *RAVIOLI, TORTELLI* AND *TORTELLINI, AGNOLOTTI*... THE PRODUCT HAS A VERY STRONG REGIONAL CHARACTER AND NO REGION FAILS TO EXTOL ITS OWN SPECIFIC RECIPE FOR FILLED PASTA: *AGNOLOTTI* FROM PIEDMONT, WHICH BECOME *ANOLINI* AND *CAPPELLETTI* IN EMILIA ROMAGNA; THE *TORTELLINI* OF MODENA AND BOLOGNA; THE *CAPPELLACI* OF FERRARA; THE *OFELLE* OF FRIULI AND VENETO; THE *PANSOTTI* OF GENOA; AND THE *TORDELLI* OF TUSCANY. HOWEVER, *RAVIOLI, TORTELLI, AND AGNOLOTTI* ARE FOUND IN ALL REGIONS WITH SIMILAR NAMES OR CHARACTERISTICS; THEY ARE OFTEN REGARDED AS GOURMET PRODUCTS WHICH ARE DIFFERENT TO EACH OTHER. TODAY, THANKS TO ARTISANAL AND INDUSTRIAL PRODUCTION, FILLED PASTA IS A FOODSTUFF WHICH LENDS ITSELF TO INNOVATIVE AND NOVEL COMBINATIONS OF TECHNOLOGY AND THE EVOLUTION OF PRODUCTION. ADVANCES IN PACKAGING (WITH AN EXTENDED SHELF LIFE) HAVE ALSO ALLOWED A WIDER DISTRIBUTION AND KNOWLEDGE OF FRESH PASTA BEYOND THE BOUNDARIES OF REGIONAL AND NATIONAL PRODUCTION.

ANOLINI
ANOLINI

Difficulty 2

Ingredients for 4 people
Preparation time: 1 h 5' - Braising: 10 h

FOR THE PASTA
14 oz (400 g) flour
2 eggs
½ cup (120 ml) water

FOR THE FILLING
10 oz (300 g) chopped lean beef
3 oz (75 g) butter
5 oz (150 g) breadcrumbs
5 oz (150 g) grated Parmigiano
1 stalk celery

1 cup (200 ml) red wine
1 carrot
1 onion
1 clove
1 tsp tomato paste
2 eggs
Nutmeg
8½ cups (2 l) meat stock
Salt
Pepper

Method

In an earthenware pot, brown the sliced vegetables in the butter. Then add the beef and the clove. Cover the meat with the red wine and a little warm water. Cook very slowly, on the top of the stove, for about 10 hours, adding the tomato paste halfway through.
At the end of the cooking time, the meat will be almost completely broken down to form a thick sauce. Prepare the breadcrumbs and then combine them together with the meat sauce, the grated Parmigiano and, if wished, the vegetables after passing them through a sieve. Then add the eggs and a pinch of nutmeg. Stir well to combine and leave to rest overnight.

Prepare the pasta sheet with the flour, eggs, and the water. Knead the dough well and roll it out as thinly as possible. At equal intervals, place small balls of the meat filling, about the size of a hazelnut, on the pasta. Fold over the pasta sheet, making sure the edges are stuck together well so that there is no air inside that would cause the anolini to burst open during cooking. Cut into small rounds, using a suitable pasta cutter. Cook the anolini and serve them in the meat broth.

Italian Region: Emilia Romagna.

CANNELLONI ALL'ETRUSCA
ETRUSCAN-STYLE CANNELLONI

Difficulty 2

Ingredients for 4 people
Preparation time: 1 h 15' (preparation: 45' – cooking: 20')

FOR THE PASTA
7 oz (200 g) flour
2 eggs

FOR THE BÉCHAMEL SAUCE
2 oz (50 g) flour
2 oz (50 g) butter
3 cups (750 ml) milk

FOR THE FILLING
7 oz (200 g) grated Parmigiano
10 oz (300 g) mushrooms
1¼ oz (30 g) butter
3 oz (80 g) gruyère
2 oz (50 g) prosciutto
Salt

Method

Put the flour on a board, make a well in the center, and break the eggs into it. Combine and knead until the dough is smooth.

Roll the dough out fairly thinly and, with the tip of a knife cut out about thirty 3-in (8-cm) squares.

Partly cook the pasta squares for 30 seconds in a large pan of lightly salted boiling water. Drain them and lay them out on a damp cloth to cool.

Place a pan onto a low heat, add the butter, and stir in the flour to make a roux. Add the milk and bring slowly to the boil to make a béchamel sauce.

Place about two-thirds of the béchamel sauce into a bowl. Finely slice the mushrooms, then cook them in a little butter with a few spoonfuls of water. Season with salt. (Alternatively, use 2 oz/ 50 g dried mushrooms. Soak them, cook in the same way, then chop coarsely.) When the sauce is nearly cold, add half of the Parmigiano and the mushrooms. Place half a spoonful of the stuffing on each of the squares, roll them up and arrange them in a single layer in a well-buttered ovenproof dish.

Finely dice the Gruyère and the prosciutto, and sprinkle the cheeses over the cannelloni. Dilute the reserved béchamel with a glass of the milk and heat through thoroughly over a low heat. Cover the cannelloni with this sauce and finish off with a layer of grated Parmigiano.

Bake for around 20 minutes at 360°F (180°C), until lightly browned.

CANNELLONI ALL'ITALIANA
ITALIAN-STYLE CANNELLONI

Difficulty 3

Ingredients for 4 people
Preparation time: 1 h 30' (preparation: 30' – cooking: 1 h)

FOR THE PASTA
7 oz (200 g) flour
2 eggs

FOR THE FILLING
10 oz (300 g) ground lean beef
1 carrot
1 small onion
1 stalk celery
1 tbs chopped parsley
2½ oz (60 g) prosciutto
¼ oz (10 g) white truffle
1 oz (25 g) dried mushrooms

4 tomatoes
½ cup (100 ml) dry white wine
1 oz (25 g) flour
Nutmeg
Salt

FOR THE SAUCE
3 oz (80 g) butter
⅔ cup (150 ml) meat sauce
4 oz (100 g) grated Parmigiano
Salt
Pepper

Method

Make a well in the flour, add the eggs, and knead the dough until smooth and elastic. Leave to rest for 20 minutes.

Roll out the pasta quite thinly and, with a sharp knife, cut out about thirty squares, 4–4½ in (10–12 cm) in size.

Partly cook the pasta for 30 seconds in a large pan of lightly salted boiling water. Drain and arrange on a moist, well-wrung-out cloth, and leave to cool.

Place some butter in a saucepan over a medium heat and add the chopped carrots, onions, celery, and parsley. Cook until lightly browned and then add the ground beef. Stir and cook for a couple of minutes to bring out the flavors and then add the chopped prosciutto, the truffle, and the reconstituted dried mushrooms; season with salt, pepper, and a pinch of nutmeg.

Cover with wine and cook to reduce completely. Sprinkle over the flour, stirring constantly, and add the chopped tomatoes with one or two spoonfuls of the meat sauce and continue cooking over a medium heat for 40 minutes. When it has started to thicken, remove from the heat, transfer into a bowl and leave to cool.

Place the filling on the pasta squares, rolling them up to make the cannelloni. Arrange them in a single layer in a buttered oven dish, cover with the meat sauce and sprinkle over the grated Parmigiano. Dot with the remaining butter and place in the oven. Bake at 360°F (180°C) for 20 minutes or until nicely browned.

CANNELLONI ALLA PARTENOPEA
PARTHENOPEAN CANNELLONI

Difficulty 2

Ingredients for 4 people
Preparation time: 55' (preparation: 20' – cooking: 35')

FOR THE PASTA
7 oz (200 g) flour
2 eggs

FOR THE FILLING
5 oz (150 g) ricotta
5 oz (150 g) mozzarella
1½ oz (40 g) prosciutto
2 eggs

FOR THE SAUCE
7 oz (200 g) grated Parmigiano
7 oz (200 g) tomato passata
2½ oz (60 g) butter
4 leaves basil
Salt
Pepper

Method

Heap the flour on a board, make a well in the center, break in the eggs, and knead until the dough is smooth and elastic. Leave to rest for 20 minutes and then roll out thinly. With a small knife, cut into rectangles measuring 4 in (10 cm) cm by 3 in (8 cm).

Partly cook the pasta for 30 seconds in a large pan of lightly salted boiling water. Drain and place on a well-wrung-out moist cloth and leave to cool.

Pass the ricotta through a sieve and place it in a bowl. Dice the mozzarella and cut the prosciutto into strips. Add both to the bowl. Season with salt and pepper, add the eggs, and stir well with a fork to combine.

Melt 1 oz (30 g) of butter in a saucepan, add the tomato passata, a pinch of salt and pepper, and the basil. Cook for 15 minutes.

Arrange the stuffing on the pasta squares, roll them up to make the cannelloni. Arrange them in a single layer in a buttered ovenproof dish and cover with the tomato sauce, Parmigiano, and knobs of butter.

Bake in the oven at 360°F (180°C) for 20 minutes and serve immediately.

Italian Region: Campania.

CANNELLONI ALLA SORRENTINA
SORRENTO-STYLE CANNELLONI

Difficulty 2

Ingredients for 4 people
Preparation time: 1 h 25' (preparation: 30' – cooking: 55')

FOR THE PASTA
7 oz (200 g) flour
2 eggs

FOR THE FILLING
10 oz (300 g) ground lean beef or pork
10 oz (300 g) ricotta
4 oz (100 g) mozzarella
10 oz (300 g) tomato sauce
⅓ cup (80 ml) extra virgin olive oil
½ cup (100 ml) dry white wine
4 oz (100 g) grated Parmigiano
1 onion
3 basil leaves
Salt
Black pepper

Method

Make a well in the flour and add the flour. Knead the dough until smooth and elastic. Leave to rest for 20 minutes.

Roll the pasta out quite thinly and, with a sharp knife, cut out about thirty squares, 4–5 in (10–12 cm) in size.

Partly cook the pasta squares for 30 seconds in a large pan of lightly salted boiling water.

Drain and arrange on a well-wrung-out moist cloth and leave to dry.

Finely chop the onion.

Place a medium-sized saucepan over a moderate heat, adding a little olive oil. Cook the finely chopped onion until it is transparent. Add the ground meat and cook to brown. Cover with the wine, cook until evaporated, then stir in the tomato paste, basil, and salt to taste. If necessary, add a little water. Continue cooking until a rich ragù sauce is obtained and leave to cool. Then stir in the ricotta, a little of the grated Parmigiano, and the mozzarella cut into small pieces.

Place a spoonful of the meat sauce in the centre of each square and roll up to form the cannelloni.

Arrange the cannelloni in a single layer in a rectangular ovenproof glass dish and sprinkle over the grated Parmigiano. Dot with knobs of the remaining butter. Bake in the oven at 360°F (180°C) for about 20 minutes. Serve immediately.

CANNELLONI RIPIENI DI CARNE
CANNELLONI STUFFED WITH MEAT

Difficulty 2

Ingredients for 4 people
Preparation time: 1 h 25' (preparation: 1 h – cooking: 15')

FOR THE PASTA
7 oz (200 g) flour
2 eggs

FOR THE FILLING
7 oz (200 g) ground meat
4 oz (100 g) butter
5 oz (150 g) grated Parmigiano
1 oz (25 g) dried mushrooms
1¼ oz (30 g) flour
2 cups (500 ml) stock
Nutmeg
Salt

Method

Heap the flour on the board, make a well in the center, break in the eggs, and knead until the dough is smooth and elastic. Leave to rest for 20 minutes.

Roll out the pasta quite thinly and, with a sharp knife, cut out about thirty squares, 4–4½ in (10–12 cm) in size.

Partly cook the pasta for 30 seconds in a large pan of lightly salted boiling water. Drain and arrange the squares on a well-wrung-out moist cloth and leave to cool.

Mix the meat in a food processor along with the butter, 4 oz (100 g) of grated Parmigiano and the dried mushrooms that have been reconstituted in tepid water. Melt ¾ oz (20 g) of butter in a frying pan over a moderate heat, add the mixture, dust with nutmeg and cook gently. In a saucepan, melt 1¼ oz (30 g) of butter, then add the flour. Add the stock and bring slowly to the boil, stirring constantly to obtain a velouté sauce. Remove from the heat and season with salt. Sprinkle over some grated Parmigiano.

Place a spoonful of filling in the center of each of the pasta squares and roll up to form the cannelloni. Butter a large ovenproof dish and arrange the cannelloni in a single layer. Cover with the prepared velouté sauce. Sprinkle over the rest of the Parmigiano and dot with knobs of butter. Bake in the oven at 360°F (180°C) for 20 minutes or until nicely browned. Serve immediately.

Italian Region: Campania.

CANNELLONI RIPIENI DI RICOTTA E SALSICCE
CANNELLONI STUFFED WITH RICOTTA AND SAUSAGE

Difficulty 2

Ingredients for 4 people
Preparation time: 1 h 15' (preparation: 1 h – cooking: 15')

FOR THE PASTA
7 oz (200 g) flour
2 eggs

FOR THE FILLING
140 oz (400 g) ricotta
5 oz (150 g) grated Parmigiano
3 pork sausages
1 egg
¾ oz (20 g) lard
Tomato paste
1¼ oz (30 g) butter
1 cup (200 ml) extra virgin olive oil
Salt
Pepper

Method

Heap the flour on a board and make a well in the center. Add the eggs. Knead until the dough is smooth and elastic. Leave to rest for 20 minutes. Roll out the dough quite thinly and, with a sharp knife, cut out about thirty 4–4½ in (10–12 cm) pasta squares.
Partly cook the prepared pasta for 30 seconds in a large pan of lightly salted water. Drain and arrange the squares on a well wrung out wet cloth and leave to cool.
Press the ricotta through a sieve, collecting it in a bowl. Add to it 4 oz (100 g) of grated Parmigiano, salt, and one egg. Combine well.

Place a small saucepan of water over a moderate heat and bring to the boil. Prick the sausages with a toothpick and add to the water.
When the sausages are cooked, remove the skins. Heat a little olive oil in a frying fan over a medium heat and fry them until brown. Leave to cool then chop them up and add them to the ricotta.
Place a frying pan over a medium heat and add the lard. After it has melted (one minute), add the tomato paste, salt and pepper, and cook for 10 minutes over a low heat.

Place a spoonful of the filling in the center of each of the squares and roll up to form the cannelloni. Arrange them in a single layer in a buttered ovenproof dish and pour over all the prepared sauce. Sprinkle the cannelloni with grated Parmigiano and dot with knobs of butter. Bake in the oven at 360°F (180°C) for 20 minutes. Serve.

Italian Region: Emilia Romagna.

CAPPELLETTI ALLA ROMAGNOLA
ROMAGNA-STYLE CAPPELLETTI

Difficulty 2

Ingredients for 4 people
Preparation time: 1 h 10' (preparation: 1 h – cooking: 10')

FOR THE PASTA
10 oz (300 g) flour
3 eggs

FOR THE FILLING
7 oz (200 g) Stracchino cheese
8 oz (220 g) grated Parmigiano
2 eggs
Nutmeg
8½ cups (2 l) meat stock
Salt

Method

In a bowl, combine the Stracchino, the Parmigiano, and the eggs. Add freshly grated nutmeg and salt to taste.

Heap the flour on a board, make a well in the center, and break in the eggs. Knead until the dough is smooth and elastic. Leave to rest for 20 minutes. Roll out the dough quite thinly and cut into squares of about 1½ in (3 cm).

On each square place a little of the filling and fold over to make a triangle, pressing down the edges with your fingers to seal. Then fold over again, taking the widest point of the triangle. With the two other corners, curl the cappelletti round your little finger so that you have a ring.

Cook the cappelletti in a large pan of meat stock that has been brought to the boil. Remove with a slotted spoon as they come to the surface. Serve.

LASAGNA AL FORNO PASTICCIATA CON PROSCIUTTO E FUNGHI
LASAGNA WITH PROSCIUTTO AND MUSHROOMS

Difficulty 2

Ingredients for 4 people
Preparation time: 1 h 30' (preparation: 40' – cooking: 50')

FOR THE PASTA
10 oz (300 g) flour
3 eggs
1 tbs cooking oil

FOR THE SAUCE
3 oz (80 g) prosciutto
5 oz (150 g) mushrooms
7 oz (200 g) ground lean beef
1 chopped onion

1 chopped carrot
1 stalk chopped celery
1 tbs chopped parsley
4 oz (100 g) grated Parmigiano
4½ oz (130 g) butter
Tomato paste
Salt
Pepper

Method

Heap the flour up on the pastry board, make a well in the centre, and break in the eggs; add the cooking oil. Combine thoroughly, kneading until the dough is smooth and elastic. Leave to rest for 20 minutes, then roll out in fairly thin sheets with a pasta machine. Cut into 3-in (7-8-cm) squares.

Have ready a large wide saucepan of lightly salted boiling water. Immerse 6-8 squares of pasta at a time. As soon as they float to the surface, remove them with a slotted spoon and lay them out on a cloth soaked in warm water that has been well wrung out. Continue until all the squares of pasta have been cooked. In a saucepan, heat ¾ oz (20 g) of the butter, the chopped onion, carrot, celery, and parsley. Fry gently until a golden color. Add the ground meat and cook until brown.
Clean and finely slice the mushrooms, add to the pan. After about 4 minutes, add the tomato paste and season with salt and pepper. Carry on cooking for 25 minutes or so.

Butter an ovenproof dish. Arrange the pasta squares in layers, covering each layer with the meat and mushroom sauce, a little prosciutto cut into thin strips, and small knobs of butter dotted here and there.

Finish off with a layer of pasta squares. Pour over the melted butter and some of the grated cheese.

Bake in the oven at 320°F (160°C) for 20 minutes or until the top is nicely browned. Serve the remaining Parmigiano to sprinkle on top.

LASAGNE AL FORNO ALLA NAPOLETANA
NEAPOLITAN-STYLE LASAGNA

Difficulty 2

Ingredients for 4 people
Preparation time: 1 h 40' (preparation: 1 h – cooking: 40')

FOR THE PASTA
10 oz (300 g) flour
3 eggs
2 tsp (10 ml) extra virgin olive oil

FOR THE FILLING
5 oz (150 g) pork sausage with truffle
9 oz (250 g) ricotta
2 hard-boiled eggs
4 oz (100 g) mozzarella
2½ oz (60 g) grated Parmigiano
1 small carrot

1 small stick celery
1 small onion
1 sprig oregano
2 oz (50 g) lard
10 oz (300 g) ground beef
⅔ cup (150 ml) red wine
¼ cup (50 ml) extra virgin olive oil
¼ oz (10 g) flour
9 oz (250 g) tomato passata
Salt
Pepper

Method

Boil the eggs in salted water for 10 minutes.

Heat the lard and the olive oil in a small casserole and gently fry the chopped vegetables. Add the ground beef and brown. Cover with the wine, add the chopped oregano, and season with salt and pepper. When the wine has evaporated, add a small amount of flour and leave to cook for a few minutes. Then add the tomato paste and continue cooking for about 1 hour, adding a little stock if necessary.

Heap the flour onto a pastry board and make a well in the center. Add the beaten eggs and the oil. Knead until the dough is smooth and elastic. Leave to rest for 20 minutes and roll out the pastry quite thinly in a pasta machine. Cut into long strips to fit your baking dish.

Partly cook the pasta in a large pan of salted water for 40 seconds. Drain and place them to dry on a clean cloth.

In a buttered ovenproof dish, arrange the pasta in layers, covering each layer with meat sauce, followed by slices of the sausage, ricotta flakes, chopped or sliced hard-boiled egg, and diced mozzarella, making sure they are evenly distributed.

Cover with a sheet of the pasta and sprinkle all over with grated Parmigiano. Bake at 360°F (180°C) for 30 minutes or until nicely browned. Leave to rest before serving.

Chef's Tips

When the pasta is immersed in boiling water it must be stirred immediately, to prevent the sheets sticking to one another.

Italian Region: Campania.

FOOD HISTORY

This is a very rich and tasty dish and is traditionally eaten on Shrove Tuesday. It is prepared with various ingredients with a high fat content which after Ash Wednesday should not be eaten during the whole of Lent.
Carnevale (Carnival) is a celebration which is typical of Catholic countries and ends on Shrove Tuesday, the day before Ash Wednesday which opens the period of Lent.
The Italian word Carnevale derives from the Latin Carnem Levare (to remove meat) and traditionally refers to the lavish meals which are eaten before fasting during Lent. For this reason, Carnival recipes, from sweets to first courses like the Neapolitan lasagne are generally rich and nourishing.

LASAGNE AL FORNO VERDI ALLA BOLOGNESE
LASAGNA BOLOGNESE

Difficulty 2

Ingredients for 4 people
Preparation time: 2 h 30' (preparation: 2 h – cooking: 30')

FOR THE RAGÙ
4½ oz (120 g) ground pork
4½ oz (120 g) ground beef
2 oz (50 g) carrot
2 oz (50 g) onion
2 oz (50 g) celery
¼ cup (60 ml) extra virgin oil
3 oz (75 g) tomato paste
½ cup (100 ml) dry red wine
Water
Salt
Pepper

FOR THE PASTA
10 oz (300 g) flour
2 eggs
5 oz (150 g) spinach

FOR THE BÉCHAMEL
8½ cups (2 l) milk
5½ oz (160 g) butter
5½ oz (160 g) flour
7 oz (200 g) grated Parmigiano

Method

Pour the oil into a pan and gently fry the vegetables over a moderate heat until they start to wilt. Add the meat and turn up the heat until nicely browned.
Add the red wine and cook until it has evaporated completely. Reduce the heat and stir in the tomato paste. Season with salt and pepper, then add water and simmer slowly for about 40 minutes.

Heap the flour on a pastry board and make a well in the center. Partly cook the spinach, drain, and finely chop. Break the eggs into the flour and add the spinach. Combine and knead until smooth and glossy. Leave to rest for 20 minutes, then roll out quite thinly with a pasta machine. Cut into long strips that fit into the oven dish.

Partly cook the pasta in a large pan of salted boiling water for 20 seconds. Drain and leave to dry on a clean cloth.
Melt the butter in a small saucepan and stir in the flour. A little at a time, add the warm milk and bring to the boil, stirring constantly, to make a béchamel sauce.

In a buttered ovenproof dish arrange the lasagna, cover with ragù, and sprinkle with grated Parmigiano, Continue layering pasta, ragù and béchamel, until you have about 4 or 5 layers.

Finish with a layer of béchamel and dot with butter. Cook in the oven on a medium heat at 360°F (180°C) for 30 minutes or until golden brown. Leave to rest for about 15 minutes before serving.

Italian Region: Emilia-Romagna.

LASAGNE ALLA GENOVESE
GENOVESE-STYLE LASAGNA

Difficulty 1

Ingredients for 4 people
Preparation time: 35' (preparation: 30' – cooking: 5')

FOR THE PASTA
10 oz (300 g) flour
3 eggs

FOR THE PESTO
1¼ oz (30 g) basil
½ oz (15 g) pine nuts
1 clove garlic
1 cup (200 ml) extra virgin olive oil
2½ oz (60 g) grated Parmigiano
1½ oz (40 g) grated mature Pecorino
Salt
Pepper

Method

To prepare the *pesto alla Genovese*, chop the garlic and basil and add a pinch of salt to preserve the green color of the leaves. When the garlic and basil have been well chopped, place them in a mortar with the pine nuts and pound with a pestle to obtain a pesto, adding a trickle of oil if necessary.
Place the pesto in a bowl and combine with the other ingredients.

Heap the flour on a pastry board and make a well in the center. Break in the eggs and add the oil. Combine the ingredients and knead until the dough is smooth and glossy. Leave to rest for 20 minutes, then roll of the dough thinly with a pasta machine. Cut into 4-in (10-cm) squares. Cook the pasta in a large pan of boiling salted water. Drain; dilute the pesto with a little of the cooking water. Coat the pasta with the pesto and serve at once.

LASAGNE ALLA PIEMONTESE
PIEDMONT-STYLE LASAGNA

Difficulty 2

Ingredients for 4 people
Preparation time: 40' (preparation: 35' – cooking: 5')

FOR THE PASTA
1 lb 2 oz (500 g) flour
4 oz (100 g) grated Parmigiano
2 eggs
2 egg yolks

FOR THE SAUCE
5 oz (150 g) butter
1 ladle meat sauce
2½ oz (60 g) grated Parmigiano
White truffle
Nutmeg
Salt
Pepper

Method

Heap the flour on a pastry board and make a well in the center. Into this add the beaten eggs, the egg yolks, and the Parmigiano. Combine the ingredients and knead until the dough is smooth and glossy. Leave to rest for 20 minutes, then roll out the dough quite thinly with a pasta machine. Cut into small strips, about 1¾ in (4 cm) wide and 3 in (8 cm) long.
Cook the pasta *al dente* in a large pan of boiling water. Drain and place in a pan with butter, the remaining Parmigiano, a pinch of pepper, a little nutmeg, and the meat sauce without tomatoes. Combine well, leave to rest to allow the flavor to develop, and serve the lasagna with generous shavings of white truffle.

Italian Region: Piedmont.

PASTICCIO DI TORTELLINI
TORTELLINI PIE

Difficulty 2

Ingredients for 4 people
Preparation time: 1 h 5' (preparation: 45' – cooking: 20')

1 lb 2 oz (500 g) tortellini
9 oz (250 g) ragù
6½ cups (1.5 l) meat stock
3 oz (70 g) grated Parmigiano
Salt

FOR THE SHORT CRUST PASTRY
14 oz (400 g) flour
3 oz (80 g) butter
1½ oz (40 g) sugar
2 eggs
1 egg yolk

Method

Once the tortellini and ragù (meat sauce) are prepared, make the short crust pastry: on a pastry board, knead the flour, butter, sugar, eggs, and a pinch of salt to combine. Leave to rest under a cloth for about 30 minutes, then roll out to a sheet about 1/8 in (2 mm) thick. Using part of this, line the bottom and sides of a wide buttered and floured cake pan.

Cook the tortellini in the boiling stock, draining them as they rise to the surface. Coat them with about half of the ragù and the Parmigiano. Place them in the cake pan, lined with the short pastry, then cover with knobs of butter, the ragù, and the cheese. Continue making more layers of tortellini, ragù, and cheese until all the ingredients are used up. Cover the last layer with the remaining short pastry, then seal the pie very well at the edges. Beat the egg yolk, adding a little water to make it runnier.

Brush the pie with the beaten egg. Make a few small holes in the top with a fork.

Place the pie in the oven at 360°F (180°C), and cook for about 40 minutes. Take out and leave to cool in the mold for 10 minutes before serving.

Italian Region: Emilia-Romagna.

ROTOLO DI PASTA AL SUGO
PASTA ROLL WITH SAUCE

Difficulty 2

Ingredients for 4 people
Preparation time: 60' (preparation: 40' – cooking: 20')

FOR THE PASTA
2 eggs
7 oz (200 g) flour

FOR THE FILLING
14 oz (400 g) spinach
7 oz (200 g) ham
Salt
Pepper

FOR THE SAUCE
1¾ cups (400 ml) meat sauce
2½ oz (60 g) grated Parmigiano
½ oz (15 g) butter

Method

Put the flour on a board, make a well in the center, and break the eggs into it. Combine and knead until the dough is smooth. Leave to rest for 20 minutes.

Cook the spinach in very little water, drain, and squeeze carefully to remove excess liquid. Chop finely using a knife or blender. Chop the prosciutto and mix with the spinach. Season with salt and pepper.

Roll out the pasta into a thin sheet and spread the filling on it, in one layer. Now roll the pasta sheet with the filling and place the roll on a cloth. Wrap it in the cloth and tie the two ends together. Place a large pan of water on to heat. When it has come to the boil, add a little salt and place the roll into the water. Leave to simmer for about 15 minutes.

Remove the roll from the pan and carefully untie the cloth. Take out the roll and slice. Arrange the slices in a buttered ovenproof dish. Cover with the warm meat sauce and grated Parmigiano.

This dish can be prepared in advance. Just before serving, place the dish in the oven for a few minutes to brown.

TORTELLI DI ERBETTE
SWISS CHARD AND RICOTTA-STUFFED TORTELLI

Difficulty 3

Ingredients for 4 people
Preparation time: 1 h 5' (preparation: 1 h – cooking: 5')

FOR THE PASTA
10 oz (300 g) flour
3 eggs

FOR THE FILLING
1 bunch swiss chard
1½ lb (700 g) ricotta
2 oz (50 g) grated Parmigiano
1¼ oz (30 g) butter
1 egg
Grated nutmeg
Salt

FOR THE SAUCE
2½ oz (60 g) butter
2½ oz (60 g) grated Parmigiano

Method

Put the flour on a board, make a well in the center, add the eggs, and knead to form a smooth dough. Leave to rest for 20 minutes.

Place a pan of water on to heat and, when it comes to the boil, add the chard. Cook, drain, and squeeze well to remove excess liquid, then chop. In the meantime, press the ricotta through a sieve, add the Parmigiano, the softened butter, the egg, and the chard. Season with salt, pepper, and nutmeg.

Roll out the pasta to form a thin sheet and cut into 3-in (8-cm) squares. Carefully place small amounts of the filling, the size of a hazelnut, on the squares and fold over to make a triangle. Close the edges by pressing down with the tip of a fork.

Cook the tortelli in a large pan of lightly salted boiling water. Drain when *al dente*, coat with butter, and sprinkle with Parmigiano. Serve.

Italian Region: Emilia-Romagna

TORTELLI DI ZUCCA
PUMPKIN TORTELLI

Difficulty 3

Ingredients for 4 people
Preparation time: 1 h' 35' (preparation: 1 h 30' – cooking: 5')

FOR THE PASTA
10 oz (300 g) flour
3 eggs

FOR THE FILLING
3 oz (80 g) grated Parmigiano
1 egg
Grated nutmeg
Salt

FOR THE DRESSING
2½ oz (60 g) butter
2½ oz (60 g) grated Parmigiano

Method

Heap the flour on a board, make a well in the center, break in the eggs, and knead until the dough is smooth. Leave to rest for 20 minutes.

Slice the pumpkin and remove the skin, the seeds, and the fibrous flesh. Bake in a hot oven, or boil in a large pan of salted water, or steam. Remove the skin and press through a sieve. Using a cloth or kitchen paper, mop up any excess liquid. Stir together with the Parmigiano and the egg to combine; season to taste with salt and grated nutmeg. Leave to rest for about 30 minutes.

Roll out the pasta to make a thin sheet and cut into 2½-in (6-cm) squares. Place a small amount of the filling, about the size of a hazelnut, in the center of each square. Fold over to make a triangle and press the edges together with your fingers to make sure the filling cannot escape during cooking. Now bring together, taking the two outermost corners of the triangle and wrapping it around your index finger.

Cook the tortelli in a large pan of lightly salted boiling water, drain when *al dente*, and dress with melted butter and Parmigiano. Serve immediately.

Italian Region: Lombardy.

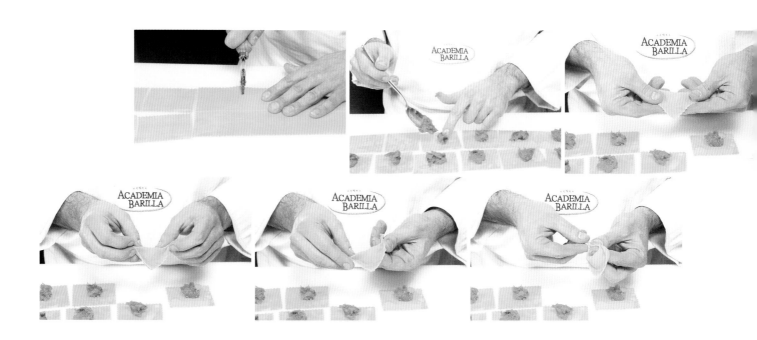

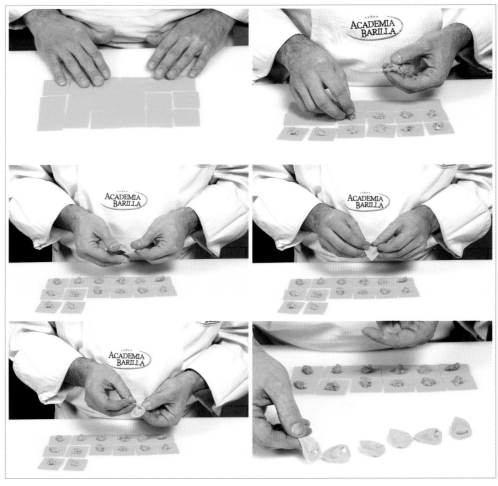

TORTELLINI ALLA BOLOGNESE
TORTELLINI BOLOGNESE

Difficulty 3

Ingredients for 4 people
Preparation time: 1 h 35' (preparation: 1 h 30' – cooking: 5')

FOR THE PASTA
10 oz (300 g) flour
3 eggs

FOR THE FILLING
4 oz (100 g) mortadella
4 oz (100 g) prosciutto
4 oz (100 g) pork loin
4½ oz (120 g) grated Parmigiano
¾ oz (20 g) ox marrow (optional)
1 egg
8½ cups (2 l) beef stock
Grated nutmeg
Salt

Method

Heap the flour on a board and make a well in the center, then add the eggs. Knead until the dough is smooth. Leave to rest for 20 minutes.

Grind the mortadella, the prosciutto, the pork loin, and the marrow jelly. Stir the Parmigiano and egg into the ground meat mixture. Season to taste with salt and grated nutmeg.

Roll out the pasta to make a thin sheet and cut into 1½ in (3 cm) squares. Place on each square a little of the filling and fold over to make a triangle, pressing down the edges with your fingers.

Now taking the top corner, fold over again. Bring the two opposite corners together, placing one on top of the other to close the tortellini, curling around your finger so that you have a little ring.

Bring the meat stock to the boil, and cook the tortellini until the pasta is *al dente*. Leave to rest for a few minutes before serving.

Italian Region: Emilia-Romagna.

SPECIALTY PASTA

Today, pasta is not just limited merely to types using durum-wheat semolina or eggs; it can also be enriched with many different ingredients. To meet a growing demand for novelty in both formats, pasta production has been gradually diversifying into a range of increasingly rich and varied colors and tastes.

A "specialty pasta" can be defined as one that in addition to water or egg introduces various flavors or ingredients: pastas with malt and gluten; wheat germ pasta (amounting to 3 per cent); pasta with water-soluble milk protein; pasta with vegetables; and pastas with edible mushrooms and truffles, natural flavorings, spices, herbs, chili paste, saffron, and, in some cases, table salt, to a maximum proportion of 4 per cent.

Belonging to this group, for example, green pasta is colored and flavored with spinach or chard, while red pasta is colored with tomatoes. There is also pasta colored with squid ink, the liquid used by cuttlefish as a weapon of defense. There are specialty pastas made either wholly or integrated and enriched with cereals other than whole-wheat flour, such as flour made from chestnuts. Or those with different origins such as buckwheat flour, which is used to manufacture the world famous *pizzoccheri* of the Valtellina valley.

These ingredients are added for different reasons: to improve the performance of the cooking process (for example with gluten or milk); through the provision of additional proteins like those already present in durum-wheat semolina; and to improve the nutritional value by the addition of proteins from milk, wheat germ or legumes, thus making the pasta a complete food differentiated by color or flavor with spices, vegetables or malt to create pre-seasoned variations. There are also specialty products — "quasi-pastas" that are made from grains which do not belong to the wheat family, for example those made with corn flour or rice.

Essentially, the specialty pastas fall into two families: those containing gluten (made with wheat, rye, etc.) and those without gluten (rice, maize, barley, oats). The latter are mainly used for dietary reasons. From the culinary point of view, all specialty pastas owe their existence to the imagination and inventiveness of their creators (in some cases through traditional recipes), and can rightly be described as real culinary innovations.

Finally in this grouping, for reasons of simplicity, recipes made with potatoes have also been included. These include products such as gnocchi (so dear to the Italian gastronomic tradition), which could not under law be described as pasta, but which are now making a name for themselves as some of the most popular first courses.

GNOCCHI DI PATATE CON RAGÙ ALLA ROMAGNOLA
POTATO GNOCCHI WITH MEAT SAUCE ROMAGNA-STYLE

Difficulty 2

Ingredients for 4 people
Preparation time: 1 h 30' (preparation: 30' – cooking: 1 h)

FOR THE GNOCCHI
14 oz (400 g) cooked and puréed potatoes
4 oz (100 g) flour
1 egg
Salt

FOR THE RAGÙ
9 oz (250 g) rump or topside of beef
2 oz (50 g) lard/ground pork fat
½ small onion
1 small carrot
½ stalk celery
¼ cup (50 ml) extra virgin olive oil
7 oz (200 g) tomato pulp
½ cup (100 ml) dry red wine
Stock (if necessary)
1 bay leaf
2½ oz (60 g) grated Parmigiano
Salt
Pepper

Method

Blend the flour into the potato purée while it is still warm, to obtain a firm but delicate and soft dough. Divide it into pieces, roll in flour, and, working the dough by hand, form into small sticks ¾–1½ in (20–30 mm) in diameter. Cut into cylindrical pieces not more than 1½ in (30 mm) long. Work through them one by one with a fork and with your thumb, squashing them slightly in the middle. Arrange them on a floured dishtowel.
Chop the celery, carrot, and the onion. Grind the beef. Heat the oil in a large skillet over a high heat and add the ground pork fat. When hot, add the chopped vegetables and cook until golden brown. After a few minutes, add the ground meat and the bay leaf. Cook for around 10 minutes until nicely browned. Add all the wine, allow to evaporate completely; finally add the tomato pulp. Reduce the heat and simmer for about 40 minutes. Add a little stock, if necessary, to avoid it drying out too much during the cooking. Season with salt and pepper.
Place the gnocchi in a large pan of lightly salted boiling water and once immersed cook for 1 minute. Drain and dress with the prepared ragù and the grated Parmigiano.

GNOCCHI DI SEMOLINO CON PECORINO ROMANO
SEMOLINA DUMPLINGS WITH PECORINO ROMANO

Difficulty 2

Ingredients for 4 people
Preparation time: 50' (preparation: 45' – cooking: 5')

9 oz (250 g) semolina
4 cups (1 l) milk
3 oz (70 g) butter
3 egg yolks
7 oz (200 g) grated Pecorino
¼ oz (10 g) thyme
Nutmeg
Salt
Pepper

Method

Place a large pan onto a medium heat and bring to the boil the milk
seasoned with salt and pepper. Sprinkle in the semolina, whisking it
continuously to avoid any lumps forming. Leave to cook for a few minutes.
When it starts to coagulate and to come away from the sides, remove from
the heat and leave it to cool down for a couple of minutes. Stir in the egg
yolks and flavor with the nutmeg.
Then add a quarter of grated Pecorino and stir in carefully.
Blend in the butter and roll out the dough on a surface greased with
oil or butter.
Brush the top of the dough lightly with butter and, on a sheet of
greaseproof paper, roll out the pasta to a thickness of ¼ in (½ cm) with
a rolling pin. Leave to cool.
With a teardrop pastry cutter, cut out the gnocchi and arrange them
on a buttered baking sheet.
Sprinkle the rest of the Pecorino over the gnocchi and brown in the oven
at 400°F (200°C) for a few minutes. The gnocchi can be accompanied by
a fresh tomato sauce.

Chef's Tips

The nutmeg must be added to the dumplings only when they have been
taken off the heat. If added during cooking its aroma and fragrance will
disappear. The semolina must be added to boiling water, otherwise it will
not coagulate.
The yolks and the Pecorino must always be mixed into the dough after it
has been removed from the heat, because otherwise they cook.

Italian Region: Lazio.

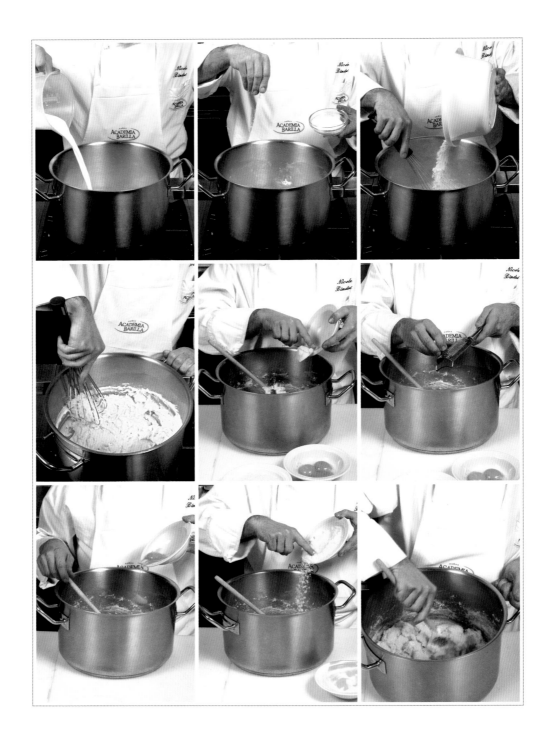

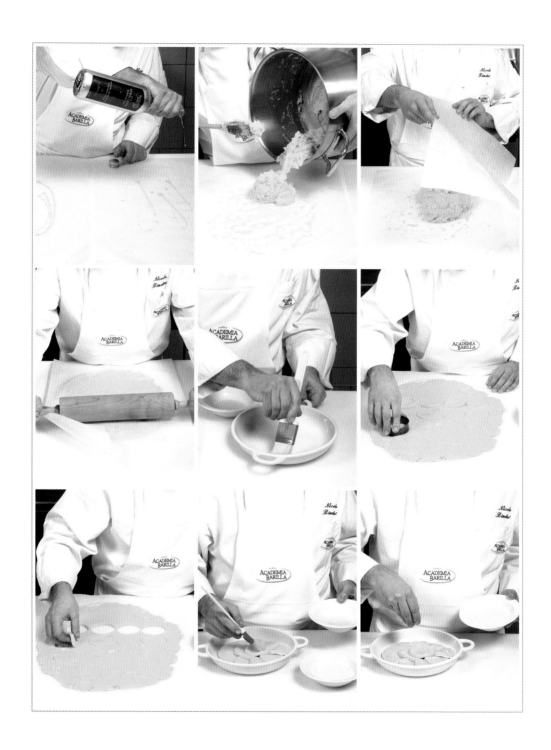

GNOCCHI DI ZUCCA
PUMPKIN GNOCCHI

Difficulty 2

Ingredients for 4 people
Preparation time: 1 h (preparation: 1 h – cooking: 10')

FOR THE GNOCCHI
2 lb 4 oz (1 kg) yellow pumpkin
4 oz (100 g) flour
5 oz (150 g) breadcrumbs
2 eggs
3 oz (80 g) grated Parmigiano
Salt
Pepper

FOR THE SAUCE
2½ oz (60 g) melted butter
8 leaves sage

Method

Cut the pumpkin into quarters and remove the seeds. Cover with aluminum foil and make a few holes in it to allow the steam to escape, then bake in the oven at 375°F (190°C) for about 40 minutes. When the pumpkin is cooked, cut the flesh away from the skin, then pass it through a vegetable mill on the coarsest setting; leave to cool. Combine with the flour, two-thirds of the breadcrumbs, ¾ oz (20 g) Parmigiano, the eggs, salt, and pepper to form a dough that is firm, but at the same time soft and delicate.

Divide the dough into portions, coat with flour, and form into short sticks with a diameter of 1 in (25 mm) using the palms of your hands. Cut across into small pieces of no more than ⅛ in (3 cm) in length. Arrange the dumplings on a lightly floured tray.

Place a pan onto a low heat, melt the butter, and add the sage leaves that have been torn into pieces by hand.

Cook the gnocchi in a pan of lightly salted boiling water; drain them when they come to the surface. Place in an ovenproof dish and sprinkle over the remaining breadcrumbs and Parmigiano. Pour over the melted butter and bake in the oven at 360°F (180°C) for 5 minutes.

Italian Region: Friuli-Venezia Giulia.

PISAREI E FASÓ
DUMPLINGS WITH BEANS

Difficulty 2

Ingredients for 4 people
Preparation time: 12 hours for soaking the beans
2 h (preparation: 50' – cooking: 1 h 10')

FOR THE PASTA
7 oz (200 g) flour
4 oz (100 g) breadcrumbs
⅔ cup (150 ml) warm water
1 pinch salt

FOR THE BEANS
7 oz (200 g) finely ground pork fat/lard
¼ oz (10 g) butter
4 tsp (20 ml) olive oil
7 oz (200 g) borlotti beans

1 clove garlic
1 small onion
1 stick celery
1 carrot
5 oz (150 g) pork rind
2 tbs chopped parsley
5 leaves basil
4 oz (100 g) grated Parmigiano
Salt
Black pepper

Method

Heap the flour onto a board, make a well in the center, and place the breadcrumbs in the well. Add salt and the water. Work into a dough, kneading until smooth. Leave to rest for about 30 minutes. Shape the rested pasta into a long snake of about ¼ in (5 mm) in width and tear off small pieces of dough, each about ½ in (10 mm) long. Then, working all the time on the pastry board, press lightly down on each bit of pasta with the thumb, to make little hollowed out gnocchi.

To prepare the beans: Place a pan over a low heat with the butter, the oil, the lard, and the whole garlic, and cook for around 15 minutes. Chop the vegetables into cubes of around ¼ in (5 mm). When the lard has melted, remove the garlic and add the vegetables. Sauté the vegetables for a couple of minutes, or until they start to color, and then add the softened beans, stirring frequently to bring out the flavor. Add 12½ cups (3 l) of water and bring slowly to the boil. Flash-fry the pork rinds and then rinse in cold water.

Meanwhile, place a skillet over a medium heat with the pork rinds and cover with water. Bring to the boil and cook for a few minutes. Remove from the pan and carefully scrape away any remaining fat. Cut the rinds into ½ in (10 mm) cubes. Halfway through cooking the beans (about 30 minutes), add the pork rinds to the pan. Finish cooking the beans, adjusting the seasoning at the end. Add the pisarei, or little gnocchi, and cook for about 10 minutes.

Turn the heat off, add half the grated Parmigiano, the chopped parsley, the basil leaves, torn roughly by hand, and stir well. Serve with the remaining grated Parmigiano.

Italian region: Emilia-Romagna.

PIZZOCCHERI

PIZZOCCHERI

Difficulty 2

Ingredients for 4 people
Preparation time: 45' (preparation: 30' – cooking: 15')

FOR THE PASTA
9 oz (250 g) black buckwheat flour
3 oz (75 g) flour
5½ oz (165 g) water

FOR THE DRESSING
10½ oz (350 g) savoy cabbage or Swiss chard
9 oz (250 g) butter
9 oz (250 g) mild Casera cheese
2 cloves garlic
4 oz (100 g) grated Parmigiano
Salt

Method

Combine the two types of flour—white and buckwheat—together on a pastry board, and form a dough with the water. Knead for at least 15 minutes until velvety to the touch. Then roll out the dough to just under ¼ in (5 mm) in thickness and cut it into strips about 2¾ in (70 mm) long. Lay the strips on top of each other and cut them into strips of tagliatelle just over ¼ in (5 mm) wide. Cut the Casera cheese into very thin slices and keep chilled in the refrigerator.

Break the Savoy cabbage up by hand into large pieces (or else cut the Swiss chard into 2 in/5 mm pieces). Place a large pan of water over a high heat. When boiling, add the Savoy cabbage or Swiss chard. After 5 minutes, salt the water and add the pizzoccheri. Cook them in fast boiling water for 7–10 minutes. Before draining, check the pizzoccheri to make sure that they are tender but not overcooked.

Then, with a slotted spoon, lift some of the pizzoccheri and greens out of the pan and place in an ovenproof dish. Sprinkle over grated Parmigiano and the Casera cheese. Continue in this way until all the ingredients have been drained and dressed. While the pizzoccheri are cooking, place a small pan onto a low heat, melt the butter with the whole clove of garlic. When the butter has melted, remove the garlic clove, then pour the butter into the ovenproof dish over the pizzoccheri and serve.

The amount of butter might seem excessive but, in this recipe from Teglio, this is the traditional way of serving pizzoccheri.

Italian Region: Lombardy.

VINCISGRASSI ALLA MARCHIGIANA
MARCHE-STYLE LASAGNA

Difficulty 2

Ingredients for 4 people
Preparation time: 1 h 45' (preparation: 1 h – cooking: 45')

FOR THE CREPES
1½ oz (40 g) flour
3 eggs
4 tsp (20 ml) extra virgin olive oil
½ cup (100 ml) milk
4 tsp (20 ml) vin cuit
1½ oz (40 g) grated Parmigiano
Salt

FOR THE RAGÙ
3 oz (80 g) butter
2 oz (50 g) flour
5 oz (150 g) prosciutto
4 oz (100 g) ground lean meat
2 oz (50 g) truffle from Acqualagna
1½ cups (300 ml) cream
4 cups (1 l) milk
Salt
Pepper

Method

For the crepes

Combine all the ingredients apart from the oil and the Parmigiano and beat to form a smooth batter. Place a pan onto a medium heat, lightly grease it, and cook the crepes until all the batter has been used up.

For the ragù

Dice the prosciutto. Place a pan over a medium heat with the butter. Add the prosciutto and the ground meat. Cook for 10 minutes or so, until nicely browned. Add the flour and cook until dry and the ingredients are lightly toasted. Add the milk and cook for at least 30 minutes. Season with salt and pepper. Add the cream and flavor with shavings of the truffle. In a buttered ovenproof dish, alternate layers of the crepes with the ragù, until all the ingredients have been used up, taking care that the last layer is meat sauce. Sprinkle over the Parmigiano and bake in the oven at 360°F (180°C), or until golden brown. Remove from the oven and allow to cool slightly before serving.

Chef's Tips

This lasagne typical of the Macerata area is so popular in the Marche region that people say there is no Christmas without *vincisgrassi*.
To make sure the dish develops its traditional rich flavor, use ingredients and typical products from the Marche region.

Italian Region: Marche.

FOOD HISTORY

Tradition has it that vincisgrassi, *a dish originally from the Macerata area, was named after an Austrian general, Windisch-Graetz, who fought against Napoleon in 1799. People say that the dish was prepared to honor him. In fact, however, this dish was apparently already included in the traditional cuisine of the area: Indeed it is mentioned, by the name of* princisgras *in Antonio Nebbia's book "Il Cuoco Maceratese" (the Chef from Macerata) as early as 1783.*

COOKING DRIED PASTA

For well-cooked dried pasta, follow these simple rules.

For each 4 oz (100 g) of dried pasta you will need 4 cups (1 l) of water and ¼ oz (7 g) of salt for the cooking.

Plunge the pasta into salted boiling water.

It is important to stir the pasta for the first minutes of cooking to avoid pieces of pasta sticking together. Follow the cooking time stated by the manufacturer. If the pasta is tossed in a sauce, it is best to drain it a couple of minutes before the time suggested on the packet and to continue cooking it in the pan with the sauce, adding a little of the cooking water.

BÉCHAMEL

Béchamel varies in thickness according to the amount of flour that is used. Here are the amounts for two different preparations using different proportions.

Time of preparation: 10 minutes

Ingredients for 4 people

Runny béchamel: Use instead of cream to lighten the dishes.
4 cups (1 l) Milk
1¼ oz (30 g) Butter
1¼ oz (30 g) Flour
Salt
Pepper

Béchamel for lasagne:
4 cups (1 l) Milk
3½ oz (90 g) Butter
3½ oz (90 g) Flour
Salt
Pepper
Nutmeg

Method: Place a pan over a medium to low heat. Add the butter and melt. Add the flour and cook for 10 seconds. Add the milk, a little at a time, stirring it in with a whisk. Little by little, the milk will thicken. Add more while stirring so as not to create any lumps. Continue until all the milk has been used up.

TOMATO SAUCE

Time of preparation: 30 minutes

Ingredients for 4 people
10½ (400 g) peeled tomatoes
2½ oz (60 g) onions
2½ oz (60 g) celery
2½ oz (60 g) carrot
1 clove garlic
¼ oz (5 g) basil
½ cup (1 dl) extra virgin olive oil
1 tsp (3 g) sugar
Salt
Pepper

Method: Wash, clean, and cut the carrot, the onion, and the celery into small pieces.

Place a pan over a medium heat, add the oil, and soften the vegetables with the unpeeled garlic.

Add the tomatoes, cut into pieces, the basil, salt, pepper, and sugar, and simmer for at least 20 minutes.

Pass everything through a vegetable mill.

MEAT SAUCE

Time of preparation: 15 minutes
Time of cooking: 2 h

Ingredients for 4 people
10 oz (300 g) meat (offal, tendons, etc.)
1 carrot
1 onion
1 stick celery
2 cloves garlic
¼ cup (50 ml) extra virgin olive oil
3 oz (80 g) tomato paste
1½ oz (40 g) flour
1 cup (200 ml) white wine

Method: Wash and cut up the vegetables into pieces about ½ in (10 mm) long. Place a pan over a medium heat. Add the oil, the garlic, and the vegetables, and cook. Add the meat and cook until well browned. Add the tomato paste and continue cooking for a few seconds. Pour in the white wine and cook until evaporated. Dust with the flour and add about 12½ cups (3 l) of water. Cook slowly over a low heat for several hours. Pass everything through a strainer and use as a sauce or to enrich other sauces.

MEAT STOCK

Time of preparation: from 3 to 6 hours

Ingredients for 4 people
17 cups (4 l) water
10 oz (300 g) beef
¼ boiling fowl or capon
1 stick celery
1 onion
1 clove
1 carrot
5 stems parsley

Method: For beef, the cuts best suited
to prepare a good stock are: the breast,
the muscle, the shoulder, rump steak,
brisket, belly, and the tail end.
With boiling fowl and capon, however,
nearly all parts can be used for stock and
in fact it is possible to use the poultry
whole, after cleaning it very thoroughly
and removing the entrails.
Pour the cold water into a terracotta pot
or into a thick-bottomed pan and place
in it the meat, leaving it to rest for 30
minutes.
In order to make a richer stock, add the
bone as well.
Then place the pan over a very low heat
and bring the stock to boiling point very
slowly, adding a little salt. With a slotted
spoon, remove the scum and the
impurities that form on the surface of the
stock during cooking.
Continue to skim the stock until it is
almost totally clear, then turn off the
heat and leave to cool. Once cooled,
return the stock to cook over a low heat,
adding the celery, the peeled carrot, the
parsley, and the peeled onion into which
you have stuck the clove, so that it can
be removed easily at the end of cooking.
Bring the stock back to the boil very
slowly, than cover and simmer
continuously over an extremely low heat,
for at least 3 hours, and longer if
necessary.
Shortly before removing the pan from
the heat, salt the stock. Once ready, filter
everything using a conical strainer.
Leave the stock to cool in a cold place,
until a layer of fat forms and
consolidates on the surface. When this
has happened, remove all or part of the
layer of fat with the slotted spoon so
that you obtain either a pure stock or
one that has had the fat only partially
removed.

Fundamental to the preparation of all
kinds of fresh pasta fillings, risottos, and
a multitude of Italian recipes, meat stock
is one of the most important basics for a
cook.

RAGÙ ALLA BOLOGNESE

Time of preparation: 1 hour

Ingredients for 4 people:
4½ oz (120 g) ground pork
4½ oz (120 g) ground beef
2 oz (50 g) carrot
2 oz (50g) onion
2 oz (50 g) celery
¼ cup (60 ml) extra virgin olive oil
3 oz (75 g) tomato paste
½ cup (100 ml) dry red wine
Salt
Pepper
Water
1 clove garlic
1 sprig rosemary

Method: Place a pan onto a medium
heat. Add the oil and, when hot, put in
the vegetables and cook until soft. Add
the meat and cook until it browns and
there is no trace of liquid.

Then put in the tomato paste and cook
for a few seconds. Pour in the red wine
and cook to reduce completely. Season
with salt and pepper, adding a little
water if necessary, and simmer for at
least 40 minutes, adding more water if
needed.
A clove of chopped garlic and a sprig of
rosemary can be added if wished for
additional flavor.

ANELLINI
Broth

ANELLI RIGATI
Broth

BOCCHE DI LEONE
Meat sauces

BRICCHETTI
Soups in general

BUCATINI
Amatriciana, sauces made with bacon, vegetables, cheeses and eggs

CANDELE
Neapolitan ragù, meat sauces

CANNELLONI
Stuffed and baked

CANNERONI
Soups, oven-baked pastries

CAPELLINI
Soups, oven-baked pastries

CAPELVENERE
Broth

CAPELVENERE A MATASSA
Broth

CHIFFERI
Tomato sauce, simple oil-based sauces, meat sauces

CONCHIGLIETTE
Light soups

DITALI LISCI
Soups with beans, vegetable soup

DITALINI LISCI
Soups with peas, lentils

DITALINI RIGATI
Soups with peas, lentils

DITALONI LISCI
Vegetable soup

DITALONI RIGATI
Soups, oven-baked pastries

ELICHE
Sauces made with meat, vegetables, cheeses and eggs

FARFALLE
Tomato sauce, simple oil-based sauces, sauces made with cheese

FARFALLINE
Broth

FARFALLONI
Tomato sauce, simple oil-based sauces, sauces made with cheese

FETTUCCELLE
Simple butter-based sauces, sauces made with cheese and eggs

FETTUCCINE
Sauces made with butter, cheese, cream

FIDELINI
Broth

FRESINE
Sauces made with vegetables, eggs and cheese

FUSILLI CORTI
Neapolitan ragù, meat sauces, ricotta

FUSILLI LUNGHI
Neapolitan ragù, meat sauces

GNOCCHETTI ALLA SARDA
Meat sauces, tomato sauces, ricotta and cheese

GNOCCHI
Tomato sauce, simple butter sauce, meat sauce

GOBBETTI RIGATI
Light butter sauce, soups

GOMITI LISCI
Neapolitan ragù, tomato sauces, oil-based sauces

GOMITI RIGATI
Tomato sauce, meat sauces, butter sauces

GRAMIGNA
Saussage-based sauce

GRAMIGNA PICCOLA
Saussage-based sauce, meat sauces

LANCETTE
Broth

LASAGNE
Rich, layered sauces

LASAGNE NAPOLETANE
Rich, layered sauces

LASAGNETTE
Sauces made with butter, cheese and cream

LINGUETTINE
Clams in white sauces, light on oil

LUMACHE
Meat sauces, tomato sauce

LUMACHINE
Soups

LUMACONI (RIGATONI)
Stuffed and baked

MACCARONCELLI
Neapolitan Ragù, meat sauces

MACCHEROTTI
Meat sauces, sausage-based sauce made with cheese

MAFALDINE
Game sauce, sauces made with cheese

MARGHERITE
Meat sauces, tomato sauce, sausage-based sauce

MEZZANELLI
Neapolitan ragù, meat sauces

MEZZANELLI TAGLIATI
Light sauces, tomato sauce

MEZZANI
Neapolitan ragù, meat sauces

MEZZANI TAGLIATI
Sauces made with meat, vegetables, eggs and cheese

MEZZE MANICHE LISCE
Tomato, simple oil-based sauce

MEZZE MANICHE RIGATE
Tomato, simple butter-based sauce

MEZZE PENNE LISCE
Tomato sauce, simple butter-based sauce

MEZZE PENNE RIGATE
Sauces made with meat, eggs, cheese and baked

MIDOLLINE
Broth

OCCHI DI ELEFANTE
Sauces made with meat, vegetables, Neapolitan ragù

ORECCHIETTE
Turnip greens, sauces made with meat and vegetables

PASTA MISTA CORTA
Soup with beans

PENNE A CANDELA
Neapolitan ragù, meat sauces, and baked

PENNE GRANDI LISCE
Neapolitan ragù, meat sauces and vegetables

PENNE GRANDI RIGATE
Meat sauces, vegetables

PENNE LISCE
Tomato sauce, meat sauces and simple butter-based sauce

PENNE MEZZANE
Meat sauces, simple butter-based sauce

PENNE PICCOLE RIGATE
Meat sauces, simple butter-based sauce

PENNE RIGATE
Meat sauces, simple butter-based sauce, vegetables

PENNETTE LISCE
Meat sauces, simple butter-based sauce, tomato sauce

PEPE BUCATO
Broth

PEPE GRANDE
Broth and soups

PERLINE
Light soups

PIPE RIGATE
Meat sauces, simple butter-based sauce, tomato sauce

PUNTALETTE
Broth

RIGATONI NAPOLETANI
Neapolitan ragù, meat sauces

RIGATONI ROMANI
Meat sauces, tomato sauce, sausage-based sauce, baked

RISI
Broth

ROSMARINO
Tomato sauce, simple oil-based sauce

SEDANI LISCI
Meat sauces, tomato sauce

SEDANI RIGATI
Meat sauces, tomato sauce, egg and cheese

SEDANINI RIGATI
Meat sauces, tomato sauce, egg and cheese, simple butter-based sauce, baked

SPAGHETTI
Fillets of tomato, simple oil-based sauce, fish sauces

SPAGHETTINI
Garlic and olive oil, clams, fish, light oil-based sauce

STELLINE
Broth

STORTINI
Soups, light butter-based sauce

TAGLIATELLE
Sauces made with butter, cheese and cream

TAGLIOLINI
Sauces made with butter, cheese and cream, baked

TEMPESTINA
Broth

TOFARELLE
Meat sauces, tomato sauce, simple butter-based sauce

TOFE
Stuffed and baked

TOFETTINE
Tomato sauce, simple butter-based sauce

TORTIGLIONI
Sauces with meat, vegetables, sausage-based sauce, baked

TRENETTE
Simple oil and butter-based sauces, fish sauces

TRIPOLINI
Sauces with ricotta, baked

TRIPOLINI (A NIDO)
Neapolitan ragù with ricotta

TUBETTI
Light soups

VERMICELLI
Tomato sauce, sauce made with butter, bacon, eggs and cheese

VERMICELLONI
Carbonara, sauces made with vegetables (turnip, zucchini, eggplant), with bacon, eggs, and cheese

ZITI
Neapolitan ragù, meat sauces, baked with eggplant

ZITI TAGLIATI
Meat sauces with vegetables, eggs and cheese

ZITONI
Neapolitan ragù, meat sauces, baked with eggplant

ZITONI TAGLIATI
Neapolitan ragù, meat sauces, baked with eggplant

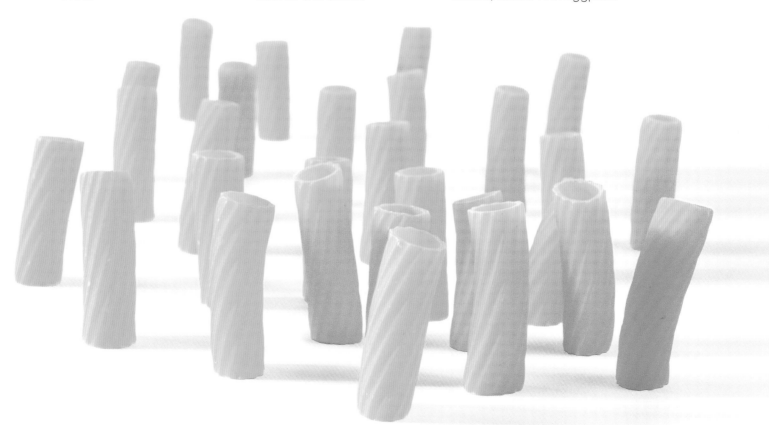

ALPHABETICAL INDEX OF RECIPES